The Book of Hatfield 1978
has been published as a
Limited Edition of which
this is

Number **602**

A complete list of the
original subscribers is
printed at the back of
the book

THE BOOK OF HATFIELD

FRONT COVER: Hatfield in 1818.

The Heart of Hatfield by Beresford Johnson.

THE BOOK OF HATFIELD

A PORTRAIT OF THE TOWN

BY

ROBERT RICHARDSON

BARRACUDA BOOKS LIMITED
CHESHAM, BUCKINGHAMSHIRE, ENGLAND
MCMLXXVIII

PUBLISHED BY BARRACUDA BOOKS LIMITED

CHESHAM, ENGLAND

AND PRINTED BY

FRANK ROOK LIMITED

TOWER BRIDGE ROAD

LONDON SE1

BOUND BY

BOOKBINDERS OF LONDON LIMITED

LONDON N5

JACKET PRINTED BY

WHITE CRESCENT PRESS LIMITED

LUTON, ENGLAND

LITHOGRAPHY BY

SOUTH MIDLANDS LITHO PLATES LIMITED

LUTON, ENGLAND

DISPLAY TYPE SET IN

MONOTYPE BASKERVILLE SERIES 169

BY SOUTH BUCKS TYPESETTERS LIMITED

BEACONSFIELD, ENGLAND

TEXT SET IN

12/14 PT. BASKERVILLE

BY BEAVER REPROGRAPHICS LIMITED

BUSHEY, ENGLAND

© ROBERT RICHARDSON 1978

ISBN 0 86023 054 6

Contents

Acknowledgements

I am incredibly indebted to a considerable number of people, in particular those who have previously delved into Hatfield's history and from whose work I have gratefully drawn. Special mention must go to the several authors of the Workers' Educational Association series of booklets *Hatfield and its People*, an exhaustive, scholarly work which was produced under the guidance of Lionel Munby of Cambridge University. Two of these authors, Henry Gray and Gladys Brown, together with Hatfield House archivist Robin Harcourt Williams, have provided invaluable assistance in reading the manuscript and their comments, guidance and enthusiasm have contributed immeasurably to the final result.

Lord Salisbury, in allowing me access to the family archives and generously permitting the publication of a number of pictures in the Cecil collection, has continued the close interest his family has long shown in the town. I am grateful for all this and for his Foreword; similarly to Michael Goldsmith of British Aerospace for the Preface.

I must also thank the management and staff of the Hertfordshire Library Service, especially at Hatfield, for their help with the special subscription facility; similar thanks are due to Mrs Greta Bishop at Gretamillie and Mrs June Walters at Gallery Four.

Denis Williams took all the original pictures and John Lingham French of Park Studios undertook copying work as well as supplying several pictures from his own collection. John Scott, Philip Birtles, Mike Hird and Simon Raynes, all now of British Aerospace, gave of their time and company records. Others involved included Dick Busby of Hatfield Library, Ken Turner of Hatfield Parish Council, Brian Lilley of Welwyn Hatfield District Council, Peter Walne and his staff at the County Record Office, Gordon Davies of Hertford Museum, Sue Harrison of the Hatfield Archaeological Society, John Gray of Hatfield Cricket Club, Ken Wright of the Commission for the New Towns, Major John Sainsbury and many others. Pictures in the parish church were taken by permission of the Rector. To all these and to everyone else who helped, many, many thanks.

Dedication

For Sheila, who introduced me to Hatfield

Foreword

by The Most Honourable The Marquess of Salisbury

Hatfield has had a long and distinguished history and if small in size has more than made up for this in the not inconsiderable number of people of distinction who have lived here.

It lies astride the old main road from London to the North, a key factor which contributed to its importance in early times. This was surely the reason why Cardinal Morton built his Palace here when Chief Minister to Henry VII, for it was close to London and on the road to his Diocese of Ely.

He was followed by Princess Mary and Princess Elizabeth, both to succeed in turn to the throne of England. After them James I came and he passed his house on to his Chief Minister. Throughout the nineteenth century Hatfield was host to many crowned heads and other distinguished visitors from all over Europe.

In the twentieth century the great De Havilland factory was among the pioneers of the aircraft industry and was responsible for some of the most famous aeroplanes in the world. Although little now remains of the Old Town, a new and thriving community has grown up around it and Hatfield continues to prosper in the present age.

Mr Richardson is to be congratulated on writing such an enjoyable and interesting account of Hatfield and its history. It will surely be greatly appreciated by those who read it, whether they live here or are visitors.

Salisbury

Hatfield

The monks who stayed,
The king who prayed,
A queen beneath a winter tree;
The soldiers strode,
The huntsmen rode,
And Pepys approved of Dr Lee.

The wickets fall,
The church bells call,
And fate is marvellous in our eyes.
The Cecils state,
The years rotate,
And Comets cross the summer skies.

R.R.

Preface

by Michael Goldsmith, Divisional Managing Director,
Hatfield/Chester Division British Aerospace Aircraft Group

One outstanding interest of Hatfield is surely the juxtaposition of ancient and modern. Robert Richardson traces its early Saxon beginnings, its continuing modest agricultural profile under the aegis of the Abbots of Ely to its first fine Tudor flowering in the benign shadow of the great house on the hill. The author has a marvellous sense of history and a great good humour to leaven it. His account of the House of Cecil as it descends through four centuries in unbroken line is a splendid tale. It is a little unfashionable nowadays to find anything praiseworthy in a system unblushingly feudal but, like it or not, Hatfield would have been a poorer and a duller place without its colourful overlords, temporal and spiritual.

I have been asked to write this preface, in a sense, as representative of another more recent aspect of Hatfield's history — for there is no doubt that the importance of our town nowadays lies in its significant contribution to the commerce of the nation. The immediate influence of London trade and the need for ever improving communications explains the eager development from horse to rail and of course, in recent years, to the enthusiastic exploitation of the aeroplane which has made the name of Hatfield world-renowned.

Apart from the design and manufacture of aircraft, which remains the town's major industry, the rapid expansion of Hatfield as a designated New Town has resulted in a vigorous and growing population of men and women who work in a wide variety of new industries. These range from light engineering, pharmaceuticals and clothing manufacture to toys and metallurgical treatments — all employ skills and commercial enterprise which would do credit to their predecessors.

The new inhabitants will, I am sure, read with relish Robert Richardson's delightfully assembled history of their forebears.

The badge of office of the chairman of Hatfield Parish Council.

Chronicles and Kings

Ten centuries ago the gift of a Saxon king established the town of Hatfield. Some six centuries later the wishes of another king made the town the home of one of the great families of England. This century the geological pattern laid down by a distant Ice Age attracted a renowned company of 'plane-builders. Around these three pivotal incidents the story of Hatfield revolves.

Lying conveniently near to London, what could have been another unremarkable country town has been distinguished by the lives of notable men and women and the movement of great events, and some fifty generations of townsfolk have passed their lives against a rich background of Church, Crown and State. Famed or forgotten, wise or witless, this long human pageant has created and maintained the eventful history which we continue today in everyday lives we consider mundane, but which our distant descendants will find as fascinating as we find the lives of those who have gone before. Every Monday is history on Tuesday.

For more than 350 years Hatfield has been the principal home of the Cecils. Their influence on the town, individually and as a family, has been immeasurable, but their treatment in these pages may appear to show some imbalance. There is a considerable amount on the 2nd Marquess, but substantially less on his son, who was Prime Minister three times. The reason is simply that the former was more active in Hatfield than the latter and those activities are more relevant to this book. In the chapter on the Cecils I have traced the descent from Lord Burghley to the present Marquess and of necessity much detail has been omitted; the bibliography indicates where this detail may be found. Where appropriate, I have included particular activities of the Cecils in the chapters dealing with those subjects; thus, for example, the Countess Anne School is briefly mentioned in the family chapter and dealt with more fully in the chapter on education.

Many volumes the size of this one would be needed to tell Hatfield's whole story. I have attempted to relate all the essential, much of the significant and some of the intriguing. From this broad outline, the reader will, I hope, want to know the rest, which will be the best result of what has been an exacting but enjoyable task.

ABOVE: The earliest written record of Hatfield. (BL) See Appendix.
BELOW: Middle Stone Age flints found in Stream Woods. (HAS)

To Begin at the Beginning

He sat in what we now call Stream Woods, a stream twisting through the trees as it does today, then disappearing underground. The trees grew more thickly then, their bark providing food for the red deer nearby. He sat shaping fragments of flint into primitive tools with which to cut, scrape, hammer and kill. He was of the Middle Stone Age and his shadowy figure may be distantly made out perhaps 7,000 years ago as the first man of whom we have any evidence in Hatfield.

The flint fragments, lost, thrown away or washed down by running water, are the clues to his presence. He was of the Mesolithic Maglemosian culture (so named after a great bog in Denmark) which stretched across much of northern Europe. In other places substantial evidence of this way of life has been found and from the handful of flints in Hatfield we may infer more. Our first Hatfeldian lived an agreeable, nomadic, tribal life hunting the red deer for food and clothing. He carried a simple elm bow and could hollow out log canoes for fishing expeditions along the River Lea. Wildfowl, nuts and berries may also have been in his diet. The woods where we find him were part of a great forest which covered much of southern England and the Continent.

Millions of years had preceded this first glimpse of man in Hatfield. During those millenia, the sea had washed over Hatfield and south-east England. Countless millions of microscopic sea creatures had lived and died, their remains gathering to form great layers of chalk on the sea bed. Over this immense period of time, Hatfield had emerged as dry land, then disappeared under water on several occasions as further marine advances laid down sand, gravel and London clay. At last another great shifting of Europe's land masses thrust southern England above sea-level again and Hatfield found itself on the eastern end of the uplands we now call the Chilterns and on the western edge of a great European plain. A long period of geological stability followed, during which the Thames and its tributaries cut their valleys through the softer rocks, laying down the basic pattern of our landscape which was given its final reshaping by the cold, remorseless power of a succession of Ice Ages. Glaciers advanced from the north, and as they retreated in the milder interglacial periods, meltwater from beneath the ice carved through the existing landscape and altered the courses of the rivers. The Thames, a tributary of the Rhine, had flowed out at Harwich; now it passed through Hatfield and on to Blackwall; now it had been pushed to its present course. At its most southerly advance the ice stopped not far north of Hatfield and water from beneath it flowed over what was to be the town. As the ice retreated again the water first flattened the surface, then deposited sand and boulder clay to form a wide, flat plain that would one day yield barley and potatoes in abundance and later would be ideal for an airstrip...

Further aeons passed. New plants like lime trees appeared as milder temperatures succeeded the freezing cold. The first rather stunted trees were replaced by more established

mixed deciduous woodland. Erosion wore away the clay in parts, exposing the bone-white chalk beneath. Hatfield is complex in its geology and its comparatively small confines present problems of description and definition. Broadly, to the north and west the chalk has been exposed and to the south and east the London clay cover has generally remained. These latter deposits laid the foundations for generations of potters, tilers and brickmakers. We are the products of all our long yesterdays.

We have as yet no evidence of man in Hatfield earlier than the Middle Stone Age which, compared to the period he is known to have been on earth, is recent. The subsequent centuries have thus far yielded little evidence to the archaeologists. Some pre-Roman Belgic pottery at Astwick, some odd fragments of broken tile and pottery and a couple of coins from the long Roman occupation of these islands: too little to indicate — as yet — any permanent or widespread habitation. There is much scepticism of the suggestion by the Reverend Jocelyn J. Antrobus in his book *Bishop's Hatfield* — the first published history of the town — that a 'fine white marble bath of Roman workmanship' found in the 19th century and still to be seen in Hatfield House indicates a Roman villa on the hill. It may not even be Roman.

If the post-Roman peoples who settled in Britain were here, we have found nothing to show for it and it is not until about AD 970, when the monks of Ely came, that we can firmly start the story of Hatfield. A century later Domesday Book recorded 'Hetfelle' (from the Saxon *Haethfeld*, meaning heath-covered open land) as having a priest and 54 families, four water mills and enough woodland to support two thousand pigs. We had begun.

ABOVE; The sole of a 14th century child's shoe found in Batterdale. (HAS) BELOW LEFT: A late 14th century iron arrowhead from Pope's Farm, (HAS) and RIGHT: a storage or cooking pot from the late 13th century discovered at Wild Hill. (HAS)

14

Let us Pray

For more than a thousand years there has been a church of the Christian faith in Hatfield. Older, darker deities may have been worshipped here, but we have no evidence and while there is a blurred glimpse of what may be Hatfield in AD 680 when the Venerable Bede records a Synod presided over by Theodore, Archbishop of Canterbury, 'at the place which is called in the Saxon language Heathfeld', is this our Hatfield or the town of the same name in Yorkshire? The proof remains elusive.

Certainly the church which dominates the Old Town can place its beginnings back to about 970 when the Saxon King Edgar gave forty hides (a hide locally varied between 120 and 140 acres) to the monks of Ely, having himself received it as a gift from his father-in-law Oedmaer. On Edgar's death some five years later the monks nearly lost it when one Aegelwin and his brothers claimed the land through a disputed agreement between their father and the late king. The law favoured the brothers and the monks had to buy back Hatfield with land they owned elsewhere. Some 60 years later the saintly Edward the Confessor confirmed their ownership.

The abundant woodland provided materials for a church, dedicated, as was the monastery at Ely, to the Saxon princess St Etheldreda, but of this nothing remains. The structure we see today is the product of many centuries, the earliest being the 13th, although there lies on the floor of the Salisbury Chapel the plain stone silhouette of a knight beneath his shield dating from the 12th century. This anonymous, enigmatic figure is the town's oldest inhabitant.

In 1108 the Abbots of Ely were made Bishops and Hatfield became one of their residences. In 1479 the distinguished statesman-cleric John Morton became Bishop and shortly afterwards started building the splendid redbrick quadrangular Bishop's Palace east of the church. Today's Old Palace is the only remaining wing. Tradition also says that Morton caused the construction of the present west tower of the church; previously the tower had sprung from the intersection of nave and transepts, but this would seem to have proved unsafe. He is also said to have widened the nave, leaving it out of line with the chancel.

William, the 2nd Earl of Salisbury, altered the church in 1618 by taking down part of the north wall to build the Salisbury Chapel. Hoarding was erected round the site to prevent morbid passers-by from staring at the corpses being unearthed. The west tower had various additions on the top, the last being a wooden spire erected in 1847 to mark the previous year's visit of Queen Victoria; notable for its prominence rather than any architectural merit, it was taken down in 1930. The nave was levelled and rebuilt with a new roof during extensive renovation in the 1870s and today the parish faces the prospect of raising some £80,000 towards the repair of the ancient fabric.

Ten bells now clamour from the tower. In 1700 there were five and in 1786 the first

Marchioness of Salisbury presented a peal of eight, but in between there may have been others. Between the 1730s and 1756 the name of the Five Bells public house changed to the Eight Bells (as it has remained) and in 1738 one J. Hutchinson wrote to the Rector, the Reverend Samuel Haynes, recommending the London bell founder Thomas Lester, as the parish was 'disposed to have a peal of eight bells instead of the five you have already'. If the pub's name reflects the ring of bells in the church, as seems plausible, there may be three bells unaccounted for. The Marchioness also gave a carillon with a tune for each day of the week, some with decidedly secular words. It remains in working order but no longer plays regularly. The bells provided an annual domestic service into this century when the churchwardens paid a man called Buff a shilling a year to ring the Pancake Bell on Shrove Tuesday to remind housewives to prepare their batter. The ninth and tenth bells were added in 1929 in memory of Rupert Cecil, one of the three sons of the former Rector, Lord William Cecil, who died in the First World War.

The recorded descent of Rectors stretches from Philip de Eya in 1228-9 through to William Todd, the incumbent since 1972, and some interesting figures emerge over the seven centuries. John Taillard or Taillor, Rector from 1500-34, was one of triplets and coupled his Hatfield living with some service to the State, now as Chaplain with Henry VIII at the Field of the Cloth of Gold, now Ambassador to the French court, now a Commissioner to decide the validity of Henry's marriage to Catherine of Aragon. Richard Lee, who arrived in 1647, is said to be the original of the adaptable Vicar of Bray, although there are other candidates; his sermon on the morning of 11 August, 1667 impressed Samuel Pepys, who heard it, as 'a most excellent good sermon which pleased me mightily and very devout'. Eight Hatfield Rectors subsequently became Bishops and William Mey, who was a layman when given the living in 1535, was ordained a year later, was deprived of it in 1554 and died in 1560 on the day he was elected Archbishop of York.

One of the longest-serving clerics in the parish was Francis Faithfull who became curate in 1812 and was Rector from 1819 until his death in 1854. Of puritanical attitude, he crossed swords with James, the 2nd Marquess of Salisbury, after telling his son Lord Robert that it was 'wicked to play at any games on a Sunday'. James wrote: 'It is my misfortune to differ with you upon the degree of strictness with which the Sabbath is to be observed' and accused Faithfull of undermining his parental authority. The Rector acknowledged the Marquess's right to bring up his children his own way, but these two strong-minded men could find no compromise in their positions. Despite these doctrinal differences, Faithfull became close to the Cecils; his son became the virtual guardian of the invalid Lord Cranborne, accompanying him on an extensive overseas tour for his health, and when Faithfull died Lord Salisbury left Hertford Quarter Sessions, where he was presiding, to accompany other members of the family and 2,000 others at his funeral.

The Cecil family and immediate relatives have provided six Rectors, the best remembered being Lord William Cecil, who took office in 1888. The second son of the 3rd Marquess, Lord Bill, as he was familiarly known, and his wife Lady Florence were popular and much-loved figures in the parish. They declined to live in the traditional Rector's home at the Parsonage (now Howe Dell School) and Lord Salisbury built them a new home, St Audrey's, in Church Street, which later became a blind home. Despite his aristocratic background, Lord William had the common touch without being patronising and was a frequent and welcome guest at the tables of his humblest parishioners. He refused to leave his beloved Hatfield until 1916, when he was consecrated Bishop of Exeter, and this kindly and devout churchman burned all the letters of condolence he received when three of his sons died in the First World War; their existence only deepened his grief. He was engagingly absent minded. Once, as Bishop, he is said to have been unable to find his train ticket at the station and when the inspector said it did not matter, as they all knew him, he replied: 'But without a ticket, how do I know where I'm supposed to be going?' Through 20 years in Exeter his affections remained with Hatfield and after his death in 1936 he was brought back to be buried where his heart had always been.

The Reverend Jocelyn J. Antrobus, who succeeded Lord William as Rector, wrote the first history of Hatfield, drawing gratefully, as have all subseqent authors, on the monumental work of R. T. Gunton, the 3rd Marquess's secretary, who spent 20 years transcribing and editing the family papers into more than 30 volumes. Having acquired an interest in the town's history, Antrobus was ready to defend it. In 1931 when the Rural District Council wanted to change the name of Back Street to Church Street he vigorously opposed the suggestion. Back Street, he maintained, was the traditional and historically proper name and he applied to the magistrates for it to be retained. The council argued that all the residents except the Rector used the name Church Street and the alteration was approved.

Generations of Hatfield townsfolk lie in St Etheldreda's and its churchyard, at rest with three Bishops, two Prime Ministers (the 3rd Marquess and Viscount Melbourne) and others of remark. They include Sir John Fortescue, who was with Henry Tudor at Bosworth Field; Sir John Brocket and his family; the Boteler family, including the splendid Sir Francis, who before his death in 1690 is said to have regularly ridden his horse up the steps of Hatfield House and through the armoury, insisting it stood on an ancient bridle-path; John Whitemore, who died in 1801 aged 103, having thus lived in three centuries; Lady Caroline Lamb, the errant wife of Prime Minister Melbourne; and James Penrose, for 25 years Surgeon Extraordinary to George III. A regal line stretching back to Edward I and including Henry VIII and all his three children may have worshipped in the church. Lady Frances Brandon, mother of the ill-starred Lady Jane Grey, was christened in a magnificently decorated St Etheldreda's after her birth at Hatfield in July 1517. The church has mothered three others in the expanding town: St Luke's in 1877, St Michael and All Angels in 1955 and the modernistic St John's, dominating Bishop's Rise, in 1960.

After the Reformation, the new Protestant religion put down deep roots in Hatfield. There was no permanent place of worship for other faiths until the early 19th century and it was the present century before Roman Catholicism re-established itself in the town.

In 1694 John Leaper's Hatfield home was certified as a place of worship for Anabaptists and over the next 150 years many other such certificates were issued, but it was 1823 before Charles Maslen laid the foundation stone of a chapel 'for the use of a Congregation of Protestant Dissenters' in Park Street. Despite only a tiny membership, the chapel survived, its Ministers sometimes Baptist, sometimes Congregationalist, and by 1925 the Park Street Chapel was the town's Congregational Church. In 1932 it moved to a new chapel in St Albans Road and since 1972 has been Christ Church United Reformed. The Chapel was demolished shortly after the move and its attendant graveyard disappeared in the 1960s when Park Close was built. Workmen clearing the site expressed concern at having to move the bodies, but agreed when a fee of ten shillings per coffin was offered; some 30 coffins were re-interred in a communal service beneath the wall of Hatfield Park, which bounds part of the Close.

There were strong connections between Hatfield and Wesleyan Methodism. Nancy Wesley, sister of Charles and John, married a Mr Lambert and lived in the town and John

Wesley preached at St Etheldreda's in 1772. But their early followers needed more than spiritual strength to establish the faith in the town. In the 1850s they began to hold services in what became known as the Moo-Cow Chapel, part of the stable of the Two Brewers public house in Church Street (then Back Street). This minute accommodation was stifling with the smell of the neighbouring cows and there was the added indignity for the teetotal Methodists of a brewery sign at one end of the building. In 1889 they moved to more permanent and less odorous premises when a new chapel costing £1,200 was built in French Horn Lane near the Great North Road junction. Fifty years later this was sold and became Tingey's furniture store for many years before being demolished as the Old Town was redeveloped. The Methodists moved to a new chapel in Birchwood Avenue in 1938 and in 1962 a second chapel was built in Woods Avenue.

Father Kenelm Vaughan came to Hatfield around the turn of the century almost as a missionary for the Roman Catholic Archdiocese of Westminster, and the brick chapel he built in the grounds of his home in St Albans Road was the first public church to celebrate the Catholic Mass in Hatfield for more than 350 years. This was superseded in 1925 when a community of Carmelite nuns built a Convent on part of the old Hatfield Brewery site and their chapel became a parish church. The nuns remained in the town until 1938, but faced an uphill struggle. One Mass in 1929 was attended by only nine worshippers, and in 1931 Cardinal Bourne, Archbishop of Westminster, told Hatfield it had the smallest Catholic congregation in Hertfordshire.

The growth of the New Town increased the numbers and in 1959 Catholic Hatfield was divided into two parishes, St Theresa's and St Peter's, the latter covering the new development on the south side of the town. The church for this new parish was completed on Bishop's Rise in 1961, a year after the Sisters of Mercy established a Convent at a house in Sycamore Avenue. Father Stanislaus Savage changed the name of St Theresa's to Marychurch in the Old Town and celebrated the first Midnight Mass in the beautiful new circular church at Christmas 1970. Ringed by vivid modern stained glass windows made by the monks of Buckfast Abbey, the Roman Catholic congregation had a new place of worship of which the Benedectine monks who founded St Etheldreda's would have been proud. Father Savage died in 1975 and his funeral service at Marychurch was conducted by Cardinal Heenan.

The surviving west wing of the Bishop's Palace, today's Old Palace,
from a drawing by Beresford Johnson.

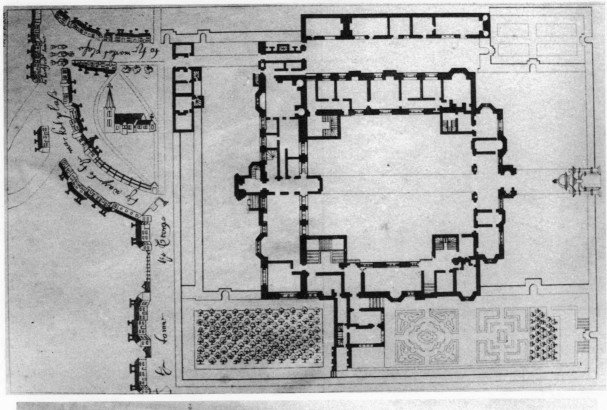

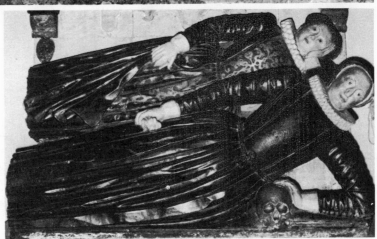

ABOVE: A plan of the Bishop's Palace built by Cardinal Morton. (CRO)
CENTRE: West view of the church and Hatfield House in 1835, drawn by
J. C. Buckler. (CRO) BELOW LEFT: The 12th century knight's tomb in
the Salisbury Chapel, and RIGHT: the tomb of Elizabeth, second wife of
Sir John Brocket, and her mother, Dame Agnes Saunders.

ABOVE: St Etheldreda's in 1806, (HM) and BELOW: the church with its
new spire in 1847.

ABOVE: The Old Parsonage, now Howe Dell School. (HM) BELOW:
Rectors of Hatfield: LEFT: Francis Faithfull, (HG) CENTRE: Lord
William Cecil, (MoS) RIGHT: Jocelyn J. Antrobus.

21

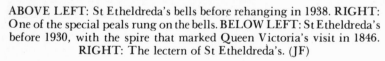
ABOVE LEFT: St Etheldreda's bells before rehanging in 1938. RIGHT: One of the special peals rung on the bells. BELOW LEFT: St Etheldreda's before 1930, with the spire that marked Queen Victoria's visit in 1846. RIGHT: The lectern of St Etheldreda's. (JF)

ABOVE: The Queen Mother and Prince Charles after attending a service at the parish church in November 1970. (WHT) BELOW: Roe Green Mission Hall, opened 1888, the forerunner of St John's Church.

23

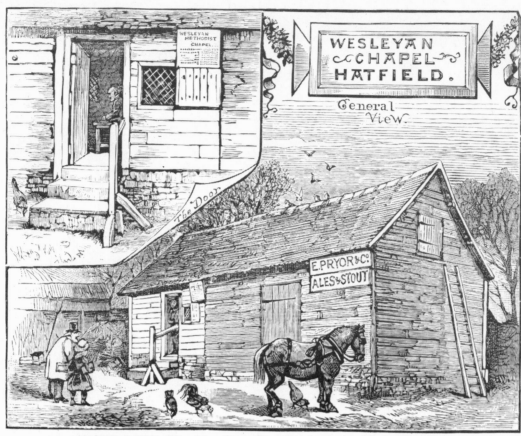

ABOVE LEFT: The Moo-Cow Chapel where the Methodists first gathered. CENTRE: The French Horn Lane Methodist Chapel, (CNT) and RIGHT: inside the Chapel. BELOW LEFT: The Congregational Church graveyard before the Park Close development. The tree in the centre still stands. (CNT) CENTRE: The building of Marychurch, September 1970, (HA) and RIGHT: Father Stanislaus Savage. (HA)

ABOVE: Elizabeth I was here. The remains of the oak under which she heard the news that she was Queen. BELOW: The Act of Parliament granting Hatfield to Robert Cecil by James I. (MoS)

First Family

The decrepit remains of an English oak mark the spot in Hatfield Park where an imperilled, imprisoned Elizabeth Tudor was told that her half-sister, the joyless Bloody Mary, was dead. With an apt quotation from the Bible on her lap — 'It is the Lord's doing and marvellous in our eyes' — Elizabeth I accepted her golden destiny and returned to the former Bishop's Palace which had been her prison. There in the Great Hall she held her first council and, with the good judgement of her father and grandfather, chose William Cecil as her Principal Secretary. A few days later she rode out to London.

For nearly 40 years she saw much of the greatest of the Cecils. Lord Burghley, as he became, was the prudent and wise minister who guided his beloved queen through the alarms, tragedies, flirtations and glories of her reign; on his deathbed she fed him with a spoon, at that moment two friends who had grown old together.

Apart from that early chance, William Cecil had no connection with Hatfield; it was his son and successor to high political office, Robert, who inextricably linked town and family. King James I expressed a desire to own Theobalds, the Cecil family home Lord Burghley had built in South Hertfordshire. He offered Hatfield and land in 12 other counties for it and the diplomatic Robert naturally agreed. To him we owe Hatfield House. Between 1607 and 1612 he built a masterpiece of English Renaissance architecture, first demolishing three sides of Morton's Palace, then, using the bricks as foundations, stamping a great letter E after the queen of happy memory on the crest of a long rising slope of land. It cost him some £38,000 and today it is priceless. For five years he watched it rising while he lived in the Parsonage, but he died the year it was completed on his way home to Hatfield from treatment at Bath. Five earls, six lords and nine knights attended his funeral at St Etheldreda's, where today the marble hand of his effigy grasps the staff he carried as Lord Treasurer of England. The carved virtues of Justice, Prudence, Temperance and Fortitude surround him. A contemporary jingle, which libellously says he died of venereal disease, recalls his reputation at Hatfield after he had fenced off Hatfield Great Wood, depriving the townsfolk of their traditional rights of pasture:

'Not Robin Goodfellow nor Robin Hood
But Robin the Encloser of Hatfield Wood.'

After his death there followed five generations of increasingly dim lights in the Cecil constellation, during which the family's influence and reputation dwindled to near oblivion. First came William, for more than 50 years the 2nd Earl of Salisbury. He entertained James I at Hatfield in 1616 spending, inter alia, £33 17s on 'Cheapside fishe and shellfishe and fresh water fishe from Cambridge'. In 1629 he completed the spoliation of the Bishop's Palace by converting the single remaining wing into stables; it continued as such for nearly 300 years.

The turbulent years of the Civil War found William bending to prevailing winds. We see

27

him upholding Charles I at York, then scuttling south to join the peers supporting Parliament in London. With his Hatfield home for the Roundhead cause and the other family seat at Cranborne in Dorset for the Crown, one feels he may have found it politic to be in the right place at the right time. But one act of kindness graces his reputation in these years. In the summer of 1647, the captured Charles I was brought to Hatfield House en route for Windsor. William allowed him to take Communion in St Etheldreda's, the first time the king had done so for more than a year. Parliament was displeased, but William may have felt some sympathy for the doomed monarch; two men were paid 18 shillings to keep guard on Hatfield Park while the king was kept there. William's fortunes fluctuated during the Commonwealth, but with the monarchy restored he entertained Charles II and a considerable retinue at Hatfield House in August 1660, when four trumpeters sounded a fanfare as the meat was served. The king's hangers-on repaid their host's generosity by stealing some of the gold plate.

William apparently nearly lost Hatfield House in 1665 or 1666 (the year of the Great Fire of London) when the household accounts record what appears to have been a serious blaze. Firefighters came from Hertford and St Albans to tackle it and for four nights afterwards men were set on firewatch. Bread and beer and tobacco were supplied to the firefighters at a cost of £2 12s 6d.

Suffering from both gout and corns, on at least one occasion William had to be carried to St Etheldreda's in a chair. It is in the church that we catch a final, devastating glimpse of him in October 1664, four years before his death, when Samuel Pepys was in the congregation and noted the presence of 'my simple Lord Salisbury in his gallery'.

William's grandson James succeeded him, his son Charles having died in 1660, and left only one tale worth the telling. In 1679 James, Duke of York, the Roman Catholic brother of Charles II whom Salisbury held should be excluded from the line of succession, was travelling north and asked to spend the night at Hatfield. James felt it best to agree, but regretted he would not be there himself; neither was anybody else. The Duke's party found Hatfield House cold, dark and empty with one bundle of faggots, a lone cask of beer and the carcasses of two small does for bodily comforts. Servants sent to nearby houses found the natives more friendly and the necessities were obtained. The Duke left a sarcastic eight shillings on the hall table as payment.

The 3rd Earl died in 1683, grieving his beloved wife Margaret, and was succeeded by his son, another James, who inherited a bad situation and worsened it. Overweight, none too bright and inconsiderate — his young bride lived alone in a decaying Hatfield House while he roamed the Continent — he became a convert to Roman Catholicism and declared his undying loyalty to James II in 1688 just before the Catholic king was forced to abdicate in favour of the Protestant William and Mary. He entertained the poet Dryden at Hatfield, which may be all he did to enhance the town's reputation, and died in 1694 aged 28.

Another James, the 5th Earl, much painted as a pretty child, continued the indifferent line, but there was a glimmer of hope for the Cecils when he married Lady Anne Tufton, daughter of the Earl of Thanet. She gave Hatfield House a long overdue spring clean and attacked the formidable problem of the neglected gardens. She also founded the Countess Anne School, a charity school for 40 Hatfield girls to learn the rudiments of domestic service, which survives in name today.

And thus to the nadir of the Cecils with another James, the 6th Earl. His reputation as the Wicked Earl has come down the two hundred years since his death, although there seems little to support the adjective. Separated from his wife for most of their married life, he lived with his mistress and children at Quickswood, a house on the family estates near Baldock, and took an eccentric delight in driving the London stagecoach. Hatfield House decayed further, some of its treasures were sold and the great foundations of Lord Burghley seemed to have crumbled forever.

But the withering Cecil line was to be enriched by marriage. After the businesslike Countess Anne came the middle-class Elizabeth Keet, whose marriage to the degenerate 6th Earl in 1745 offended society. But this lady of decidedly inferior social rank was her husband's superior in intelligence, decorum and plain good sense. After their separation, she brought up their children in London and when the 6th Earl died in 1780 there was a son, another James — the Cecils respected tradition — who would start the recovery. He was created Marquess in 1789, became George III's Lord Chamberlain, a Knight of the Garter and was Lord Lieutenant of Hertfordshire for more than 50 years. But this stabilising and worthy Cecil shows fitfully beside the charisma of his wife, the most flamboyant Lady Salisbury of them all.

If her two predecessors brought amelioration, Lady Emily Mary Hill, daughter of the Irish Earl of Downshire, added sparkle. High-spirited and High Tory (as all the family became), this vivid woman illuminated her glittering world to her death. Whether tossing gold coins to the tenantry from her carriage, being rowed on the Broadwater (the artificial widening of the River Lea in Hatfield Park) on a barge manned by twelve men in livery, or entertaining the greatest in the land, Lady Salisbury had style. As first Mistress of the Hatfield Hounds, she tirelessly hunted across Hertfordshire; two chases in one day covered forty miles and of the eighty who began the hunt only nine finished — with Lady Salisbury leading them. Her Sunday concerts at Hatfield House emptied St Etheldreda's and her card-playing evenings left the floor smothered in discarded packs. Her pinmoney for one year was £600. Her husband's death in 1823 (five thousand attended his funeral after his body had lain in state for two days) did nothing to diminish her energies and Old Sarum, as she was nicknamed, flaunted convention and defied age to the last. Turned eighty and with her sight failing, she still hunted, accompanied by a groom who would shout 'Damn you, my Lady, jump!' as they reached an obstacle — and over she went, unsteadily but splendidly.

In 1835 her death was as spectacular as her life. In late November the family had returned to Hatfield from London for Christmas. Another James was now 2nd Marquess and had married the wealthy heiress Frances Mary Gascoyne. On the night of the 27th, Lady Emily was in her room writing letters. The two candles on the kidney-shaped table were insufficient for her fading sight and she told a maid, Elizabeth Nutting, to bring a third from her bedside. The maid left her writing. At half past five the housekeeper burst into Lord and Lady Salisbury's apartments to say that the Dowager's room was ablaze. Lord Salisbury dashed into the West Wing and had to be restrained by Perugini, the house confectioner, from entering his mother's flame-filled room. As books, paintings and other valuables were carried out into the rain, the fire engulfed the wing. Lord Salisbury directed the battle as engines from St Albans, Barnet and London arrived to help, but the flames relentlessly spread and it seemed the great house was doomed. Only a change of wind and the bursting of a lead water tank in the roof saved it. The mercurial Lady Emily had perished, terribly but magnificently, in wind-tossed flames against a winter sky. It was more than two weeks before any of her remains were recovered from the blackened ruins.

One incident surrounding the fire is intriguing. The 2nd Marchioness had become a close friend of the Duke of Wellington. There is no evidence of anything improper in this relationship between a cultured young woman and the rigorously correct man old enough to be her father, but Frances later noted in her diary that at one moment during the fire she became convinced that the entire house would be destroyed, and added: 'I went to my room and took all the things the Duke had ever given me.' She died four years later and Wellington was among her mourners.

The vigour of Lady Emily passed on to her son, the 2nd Marquess, who after his marriage took the joint surname Gascoyne-Cecil, which persists as the family name. For more than 40 years this lively, busy, dictatorial man was ever-active in the affairs of Hatfield. Education, agriculture, the poor, the new railways, Sunday observance, the military, law enforcement, the shortcomings of the postal service: all this and more engaged his interest. He built the Royal Tennis court and planted the yew maze in the park and, having rebuilt the incinerated West Wing, restored the interior of the rest of the house in Jacobean style. In 1846 he entertained Queen Victoria and Prince Albert, when Fore Street was 'one continuous avenue of leaves and flowers' and a 100 stone ox was roasted and distributed to the poor. After the visit Hatfield House was open for two days and thousands flocked through to see where the Queen and Consort had slept and banquetted.

The 2nd Marquess took an active interest in his children's education, although with plain speaking as much as with sympathy. When his second son Robert (who was to succeed him) wrote home complaining of being bullied at Eton, his father advised him to challenge the first boy who started it to a fight. He acknowledged that Robert would probably be given a thrashing, but added sanguinely: 'You will not be much worse off than you are now, for you are licked without fighting.' He died just before his 77th birthday in 1868, eminently content with all he had done at Hatfield and convinced in his High Tory heart that the end of civilisation was near.

He had 12 children by his two wives (Lady Mary Catherine Sackville-West was the second) but his eldest son James was an invalid and died before him. Thus it was the unhappy schoolboy Robert who became the 3rd Marquess and the great flowering of the Cecil Renaissance. Between that disconsolate childhood and renowned old age, he was Prime Minister three times and one of the leading statesmen of the later Victorian age. His national and international activities left him little time to devote himself to Hatfield as his father had done, but his distinction in office made Hatfield House again one of the great centres of power. He had his own waiting room built at Hatfield Station and his own train to take him to and from London. He installed electric lights in the house (his father had looked at the idea in 1855) although the results were somewhat alarming: the primitive wiring in the ceiling would frequently spark alight, to be extinguished by the family throwing cushions at it. Lord Robert's serious, instrospective nature was speckled with humour and touches of the eccentric; visitors to Hatfield House would suddenly hear his disembodied voice reciting nursery rhymes as he tested the intercom telephone he had had installed. He was elected Chancellor of Oxford University and his photograph in his robes, accompanied by two of his sons, was taken by Lewis Carroll, who became a regular visitor at Hatfield House, entertaining the children with stories. The figure of Lord Robert energetically pedalling his tricycle along the asphalt paths he had laid in Hatfield Park is still remembered, and his brooding bronze statue contemplates the railway his father allowed through, from its position outside what is now the main entrance to his home; the gates were moved back several yards to accommodate it. At his death in 1903 his second son, Lord William Cecil, Rector of Hatfield, led the prayers for his soul.

James, the eldest of Lord Robert's five brilliant sons (there were also two gifted daughters), succeeded to the title. His political career, while distinguished, did not equal his father's, but his correct and conscientious behaviour won him a reputation for both wisdom and compassion. His marriage to Lady Cicely Alice Gore was a happy and advantageous partnership that lasted 60 years to his death. One early story demonstrates the couple's sense of propriety. In 1909 they entertained Edward VII and Queen Alexandra at Hatfield, but refused to invite a lady of uncertain moral character who was currently the fancy of Edward's ever-roving eye. Fore Street was again bedecked and loyal crowds cheered, but the king was put out for the whole weekend.

The 4th Marquess and his wife showed a constant interest in their Hatfield properties and tenants, many of whom were invited to join the celebrations of their Golden Wedding in 1937. Lord Salisbury restored what remained of the Bishop's Palace to its former glories, opened Hatfield House and Park to raise money for local charities and served on the County Council. In the Second World War part of Hatfield House was turned into a military hospital and its elegant rooms were lined with beds of wounded.

Active to the last, Lord Salisbury collapsed while making a speech as head of a delegation to the Archbishop of Canterbury, urging him to lead the battle against 'post-war materialism and irreligion'; he died a few days later on 4 April 1947. Lady Alice, who was to live another eight years, soon left Hatfield, a family home rendered meaningless by the death of her beloved Jem.

The political edge of the Cecils was steel hard in Robert, the 5th Marquess. Behind the diffident, rather shy man lay unswerving resolution, unshakeable principle and a long inheritance of power. He served in Churchill's War Cabinet before entering the Lords in 1941 under one of his father's other titles. From 1942 to 1957 he was Leader of the Conservatives in the Lords and when Anthony Eden resigned as Prime Minister in 1957 there was an echo of earlier centuries when the second Queen Elizabeth called on the 5th Marquess for advice on his successor, as the first Elizabeth had so often turned to Lord Burghley for guidance.

Like his brother, Lord David Cecil, the distinguished writer, the 5th Marquess took a close interest in his family history and did much work on the superb archives at Hatfield. A slightly-built man of great charm and courtesy, he maintained the interest in his Hatfield properties that his parents had shown and was regarded with much the same affection. The House and Park were opened to the public on a commercial basis in his lifetime — Hatfield is now one of the ten most popular stately homes in England — but nothing could shake the unique relationship, at once respectful and familiar, between the town and the family. He was once seen walking in the Park in somewhat shabby attire, not in keeping, as someone observed, with his status as Lord Salisbury. An old resident commented: 'Ah, but you must remember, this is his back garden'. In February 1972 the bells of St Etheldreda's rang a half muffled peal to mark his death and the close of another chapter in the story of Hatfield's first family and political England.

Robert, the eldest and only surviving son, became the 6th and present Marquess. He was MP for Bournemouth West from 1950-54, but his assessment is a matter for future historians as the Cecils continue. Robert, now Lord Cranborne and next in succession, was born in 1946 and his first son, another Robert, was born on 18 December 1970 the great-great-great-great-great-great-great-great-great-great-great-great grandson of that distant Robert who built Hatfield House.

ABOVE: The 1st Earl's tomb in the Salisbury Chapel of St Etheldreda's.
CENTRE: William Cecil, Lord Burghley, (CRO) and BELOW: Robert,
1st Earl of Salisbury. (CRO) LEFT: William, 2nd Earl of Salisbury. (MoS)
RIGHT: James, 3rd Earl of Salisbury. (MoS)

James, 4th Earl of Salisbury, with his sister, Lady Catherine. (MoS)

ABOVE LEFT: James, 5th Earl of Salisbury. (MoS) RIGHT: James, 6th Earl of Salisbury. (MoS) BELOW LEFT: James, 7th Earl and 1st Marquess of Salisbury. (CRO) RIGHT: James, 2nd Marquess of Salisbury. (CRO)

ABOVE LEFT: Robert, 3rd Marquess of Salisbury, aged 30. (CRO)
RIGHT: The 3rd Marquess as Chancellor of Oxford University with his
sons James and William. Photograph by Lewis Carroll. (MoS) BELOW
LEFT: The Prime Minister and elder statesman. (CRO) RIGHT: The 3rd
Marquess on his tricycle in 1901. (CRO)

ABOVE: The unveiling of the statue to the 3rd Marquess in October 1906.
BELOW: The statue by George Frampton.

36

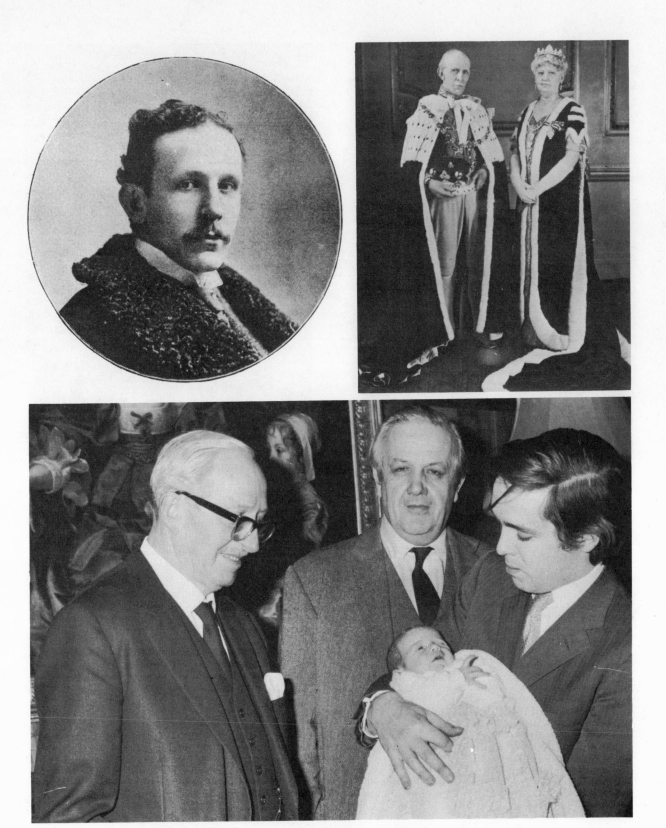

ABOVE LEFT: James, 4th Marquess of Salisbury, at the time of
succeeding to the title. (CRO) RIGHT: The 4th Marquess and Lady Alice:
a Golden Wedding photograph. BELOW: Four generations of Cecils:
from left, Robert, 5th Marquess (died 1972), Lord Cranborne, now 6th
Marquess, and Robert, now Lord Cranborne, holding his eldest son,
Robert. (AVG)

ABOVE LEFT: Lady Emily, 1st Marchioness of Salisbury, (HM) and
RIGHT: Lady Frances Mary Gascoyne, 2nd Marchioness. (CRO)
BELOW: The west wing of Hatfield House after the 1835 fire. (MoS)

38

ABOVE: In Hatfield Park in the 19th century. BELOW: A Hatfield Park
garden party in the time of the 3rd Marquess. (HM)

39

ABOVE LEFT: East view of Hatfield House in 1835 by J. C. Buckler.
(CRO) RIGHT: The south front. BELOW LEFT: Fore Street decorated
for the visit of Queen Victoria and Prince Albert in 1846, (CRO) and
RIGHT: the London Road decorated for the visit of Edward VII and
Queen Alexandra in 1909.

41

ABOVE: Hatfield from the London Road before 1847. BELOW: Hatfield
after 1847, from the railway.

The Great Roads North

The vast network of arrow-straight roads which carried the Roman rule throughout Britain by-passed Hatfield. With Ermine Street striding northwards through eastern Hertfordshire and Watling Street passing through Verulamium, Hatfield was left with only one minor north-south route which crossed the River Lea at the Cecil Sawmill. Others are suspected, but neither the ancient records nor present-day archaeology can give the town a place of importance in the Empire. The Saxons may have walked a winding 'herepaeth' along the line of Green Lanes and Roe Green Lane and the demands of the Bishops of Ely from their Palace at Hatfield would have created some traffic from London, but it is not until the 17th century that we find a road of importance passing through the town and from then on it has always been the 'Great' road to the north.

Pepys recorded his travels along this in the 1660s, pausing on various occasions to worship at St Etheldreda's, dine 'very well and mighty merry' at a local inn and admire Lord Salisbury's gooseberries. He says nothing of the quality of the road, but in the following century Daniel Defoe described this pot-holed, dung-stinking, dusty (in summer), mud-sticky (in winter) road as a 'most frightful way'. Despite these shortcomings, the demands of an increasingly mobile population made this principal route from London to York and beyond to Scotland well used. Night and day, coaches rattled along it, carrying mail and passengers, and in 1801 several companies advertised daily coaches setting off as early as 5.00am from London to Hatfield, as well as a regular cart service. By this time the Galley Corner Turnpike Trust (founded 1730) was in operation and had shifted the ancient line of the road through Hatfield Park slightly westward to run through Millwards Park. It passed the east end of St Etheldreda's, where the Cecil family graves now lie, turned sharp left down Fore Street, bent north again at the bottom of the hill to cross the St Albans to Hertford road and go on to Lemsford. There was a tollgate at Jack Oldings corner. The Trust maintained the road, which had previously been the responsibility of separate parishes and landowners; Defoe's description and the court records of actions against them for not carrying out repairs show that they were none too conscientious in their duties. The steep incline of Fore Street presented problems and on one occasion 16 horses were needed to haul up the York wagon; coming down, the wooden brake had to be held hard on to keep things under control. The practical James, 2nd Marquess of Salisbury, experimented with wooden blocks in the road to give a better grip to the wheels, which had to be of a mimimum width or an additional charge was imposed. In 1839 the Trust collected a record £1,880 in tolls; its demise and that of the stagecoach was ensured by the coming of the railway.

The 2nd Marquess is generally credited with having the vision to welcome the railway enthusiastically, but the earliest correspondence he had on the matter shows at best an ambivalent attitude, coupled with some hostility to the idea. Perhaps he was deliberately cool to win eventually greater advantage for himself. Whatever his motives, in October 1844 he commented that he 'could not look with much satisfaction to the making of a railroad through the parish', but finding that the railway companies 'who intend to intrude on our retirement' were serious, he agreed to discuss the proposals with his neighbours to decide what attitude they should adopt. After much negotiation, work started about 1847 and it was reckoned that one police superintendent and three constables would be enough to keep order among the 250 workmen who would live in Hatfield for the 18 months the work would take. In May of that year Lord Salisbury wrote to the Great Northern Railway Company complaining that a great number of men were working on his land and 'as you are so poor I must be paid before you take possession'. Robert Baxter, the company's solicitor, drily replied that the company was not poor, but if it was, the Marquess's insistence on immediate payment 'would be a peculiar course of relief'.

Lord Salisbury negotiated the moving of the Great North Road off his land at this time to follow the route of the present A1000; he was the contractor, with the railway company paying £8,000 towards the cost. The relationship between the two sides remained prickly; six months after the line through Hatfield opened on 7 August 1850, Lord Salisbury was successfully prosecuted by the railway company for obstructing the old road before the new one was completed. Having ensured that the new redbrick station was built conveniently near Hatfield House (although the entrance to the park which now stands opposite the station was not built in his time), the 2nd Marquess continued active in promoting his own interests as branch lines were proposed to Hertford and St Albans. The line to the north had a bad start with an accident the month after the opening; a year after the opening, in August 1851, Queen Victoria travelled by train through the town en route for Balmoral.

One social consequence of the earlier road traffic was the abundance of pubs in Hatfield, at that time a small, compact town clustered about St Etheldreda's, which was a convenient stopping place out of London. In today's Old Town only the Salisbury Hotel, Eight Bells, Horse and Groom and Hatfield Arms (previously the Great Northern and before that the Douro Arms) remain out of some 25 in the area. The Eight Bells, formerly the Five Bells, is the town's oldest pub and claims Bill Sykes, the villain of Oliver Twist, among its imaginary customers. Charles Dickens, who came to Hatfield as a newspaper reporter to cover the fire which killed the first Marchioness of Salisbury, stayed at the Salisbury Arms at the top of Fore Street. The building is now converted into flats, but the bricked-up archway through which the stagecoaches passed remains visible; Byron's body lay there overnight as his cortege took him for burial at Newstead Abbey, and his mistress Lady Caroline Lamb is buried with her husband, Prime Minister Lord Melbourne, in St Etheldreda's opposite. The Dray Horse, which stood near the bottom of Church Street, enterprisingly cashed in after Edward VII sat on a beer barrel in Hatfield Brewery yard while his car was repaired in the early years of the century: that same night it displayed a barrel with the legend 'King Edward VII sat here' and business boomed — but the following night nearly every other pub in the town had a barrel with a similar claim. The Salisbury Hotel was originally a Temperance Hotel and a popular stopping place for cyclists; one Sunday in 1898 a thousand of them pedalled past Barnet church in an hour, heading for Hatfield.

The George Inn stood at the top of Church Street, facing the Old Palace across what was then the main London Road. This substantial and important building is first recorded in the 1540s and about a century later was the scene of a strange legendary encounter between the highwayman James Hind and a beggar woman who gave him a little box 'almost like a

Sun-Dyal'. This, she told him, would show him the way out of any danger he was in, but it would only last for three years. After that Hind should return to her and she would 'renew the Verteu of this Charm again'. Three years later in 1649 Hind was wounded in Ireland. He later returned to England, but it is not known if he came back to Hatfield to find the woman again; possibly not, as he was executed in 1651. There was an odd echo of the tale in 1974 when the Hatfield Archaeological Society, excavating the site of the George, found the face of a compass-like device of the same period. Perhaps another of the strange woman's talismans?

In today's New Town, the Robin Hood (since rebuilt), Boar and Castle, White Lion and Gun appeared on the St Albans Road in 1850 as the railway caused development west of the Old Town. Established residents nicknamed this new community California and may have considered it as remote and exotic as the Americas, but events over the next 100 years gradually shifted the industrial and commercial enterprise of Hatfield to the expanding New Town, leaving Old Hatfield a mainly residential area. The road pattern followed this movement. The A1000 was superseded in 1927 by the opening of the Barnet by-pass — the A1 — which joined the older Great North Road at what is now Jack Oldings roundabout. In 1966 the A1000 was severed when the bridge over the railway near the Wrestlers pub collapsed and was never re-opened to road traffic. In 1972 some 300 yards of the A1000 were re-routed slightly at the new roundabout at Gray's garage and what had been the busy thoroughfare of Brewery Hill became part of the new Salisbury Square shopping precinct. The high-speed Barnet by-pass achieved a sinister reputation in the 1950s when the horn player Dennis Brain, and Michael Ventris, who deciphered the Linear B alphabet of the Mycenaeans, were among its accident victims.

The occasional milestones still found in Hatfield giving the mileage to Reading date from 1757, when another Turnpike Trust was formed linking the two towns. Legend has it that the 6th Earl of Salisbury helped establish it to open a more convenient route to Bath for treatment for his gout, but there is no proof; there are, however, no other obvious explanations for wanting to link the towns. The road is now the A414 to St Albans.

From being an important stopping place for the stagecoach traveller and the site of a large railway marshalling yard, Hatfield has become just another landmark on the commuter's journey. Electrification of the main railway line into London was completed in 1976 and the next year plans were announced for a £20 million scheme to drive the A1 underground between Jack Oldings roundabout and a point just south of the Comet roundabout, completing a stretch of motorway standard road. Thus both road and rail traveller will pass through the town with the maximum speed and the minimum inconvenience. The older great roads to the north will carry only local traffic and in the great commerce of the nation Hatfield will be largely by-passed, as it was in the days of Rome.

Three views from Brewery Hill, the latest in 1967.

Everybody's doing it at Hatfield.

ABOVE LEFT: Hatfield postcard with a seaside flavour from the early days of motoring. (JF) RIGHT: The approach to Hatfield from London early this century, and BELOW: The Broadway past the Dray Horse.

ABOVE: The Toll House that stood at Oldings Corner. BELOW: The first
AA village sign, erected in Hatfield in the winter of 1907. (Au)

ABOVE: Pedal power for sale in Fore Street. BELOW: The London Road
past the Red Lion. (MS) INSET: The East Indian Chief, a pub for nearly
200 years, seen from the Rectory garden. (JFl)

49

ABOVE: The Rose and Crown (Nos. 40-42 Fore Street) in 1745, said to have been used by Dick Turpin. BELOW: Highwayman James Hind with the beggar woman. (HAS)

ABOVE: The Eight Bells, where Turpin is also reputed to have stayed.
BELOW: The Wrestlers about 1913, with landlord Osborn Fentiman and
his wife, three sons and customers. (AL)

51

The Robin Hood on the St Albans Road about 1900, with landlord Daniel
Howard and his family. (HG)

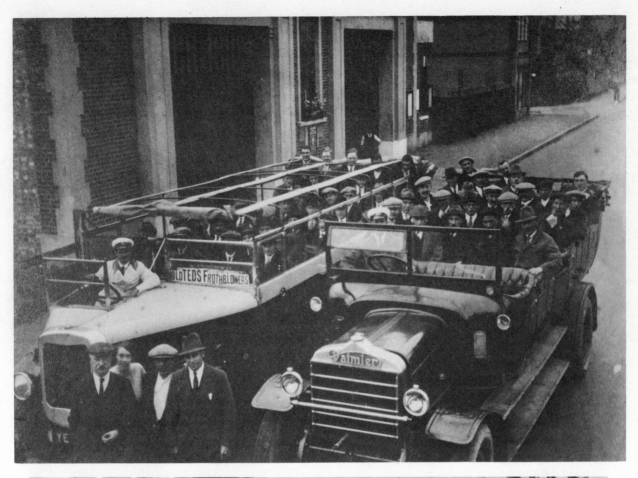

ABOVE: A coach outing from the Rising Sun in the 1930s. BELOW:
Inside Hatfield 'bus garage in the 1930s.

ABOVE: Lord Salisbury's waiting room, (CNT) and BELOW: Hatfield
station.

The Planemakers

Going about their business one day in the late 1920s, the people of Hatfield saw a single De Havilland Moth droning northwards over the town; it was a flight that was to change their history. The pilot was looking for a suitable site for an airfield and saw the great plain, the legacy of a distant Ice Age, that stretched west of the town. It looked, and indeed proved ideal.

Geoffrey (later Sir Geoffrey) de Havilland had flown his first self-built 'plane in 1909. It crashed. He rebuilt it and flew again and spent the next half century in the forefront of manned flight. The first ten 'planes to carry the famous DH classification he designed during the First World War while chief designer and test pilot with the Aircraft Manufacturing Company. In 1920 he formed the De Havilland Aircraft Company based at Stag Lane, Edgware, and started producing a family of 'planes including the renowned Moth series. As London expanded, he began to look for a new base and decided on a site on the edge of the parish of Hatfield. The company bought Roe Hyde and Harpsfield farms and in July 1934 Geoffrey de Havilland flew from Stag Lane for the last time, to touch down at Hatfield.

The London Aeroplane Club, which had been based at Stag Lane, was the first arrival in the summer of 1930. Inevitably its activities prompted complaints about aircraft noise and one correspondent wrote disparagingly in the Welwyn Times: 'Aeroplanes are not at present a feasible commercial proposition and probably never will be; they are in fact the noisy playthings of a few wealthy men and women'. Three years later the Hatfield Rural Council began building houses on Birchwood Farm as homes for the aircraft workers who were moving in; the playthings had become the engines of change.

Hatfield has been the birthplace of some 20 'planes, including two of the most famous in the history of aviation. The company has grown from a 1935 workforce of 1,752 to a wartime peak of more than 7,300 and employs some 3,500 today. The prosperity of the town has depended enormously upon its fortunes. It has made Hatfield internationally known and has added a Space Age dimension to 1,000 years of history.

The first of those 20 'planes was the Hornet Moth, a further development of the established line. The next, which captured the public imagination, began with a remark by Geoffrey de Havilland in January 1934: 'You know, we can't stand by and let this race be won without any British effort'. The race was the England-Australia air race scheduled for 20 October of that year to mark the centenary of the State of Victoria, and at the time he spoke, de Havilland had nothing that could compete. Within nine months the DH88 — the Comet Racer — had been designed and built; the first flew from Hatfield on 8 September. Eventually three entered the race, one flown by James Mollison and his wife Amy — the famed Amy Johnson who in 1930 had made the first solo flight by a woman from England to Australia in a De Havilland Gipsy Moth. But it was the Comet piloted by

1
2
5
6
9
10
13
14
17
18
19

1. The DH87 Hornet Moth. 2. The DH88 Comet Racer. 3. The DH89
Dragon Rapide. 4. The DH90 Dragonfly. 5. The DH91 Albatross. 6. The
DH92 Dolphin, a Dragon Rapide with retractable undercarriage only
built in prototype. 7. The DH93 Don. 8. The DH94 Moth Minor. 9. The
DH95 Flamingo, the first all metal airliner. 10. The DH98 Mosquito T3.
11. The DH100 Vampire, the first jet fighter. 12. The DH103 Hornet

56

fighter. 13. The DH104 Dove. 14. The DH106 Comet airliner. 15. The
DH108 Swallow, the experimental plane in which Geoffrey de Havilland
was killed. 16. The DH110 Sea Vixen. 17. The DH112 Venom night
fighter. 18. The DH114 Heron. 19. The DH121 Trident in Chinese livery.
20. The DH125 executive jet.

Tom Campbell Black and Charles Scott that won, hopping round half the planet in 70 hours, 54 minutes and 18 seconds. Of the flight, Scott memorably said later: 'It was lousy — and that's praising it'. Only five DH88s were built (the winning 'plane is now in the Shuttleworth collection) and they are commemorated in Hatfield today by the Comet Hotel, built in 1936 with a model of the 'plane as its sign.

The glamorous adventure of the Comet Racer and the growing success of the company with three King's Cup Air Races being flown from Hatfield (Geoffrey de Havilland won in 1935, flying against two of his three sons, Geoffrey and John) gave way to the serious prospects of war. Unhappily, de Havilland planned a new warplane, an all-wooden two-man aircraft powered by Rolls Royce Merlin engines. Its secret would be speed, making a rear gunner unnecessary. When he put the idea to the Air Ministry in 1937 an official told him: 'Forget it. You people haven't produced a new war machine for years'. Disgusted but undeterred, he went ahead with the design work at Hatfield under the direction of the company's chief designer, Ronald E. Bishop. Official approval eventually came from Air Marshal Sir Wilfrid Freeman when he was appointed Chief Executive at the Air Ministry. Some wit dubbed the project Freeman's Folly; the Luftwaffe never saw the joke.

The 'plane that first flew from Hatfield on 25 November 1940 became legendary: the Mosquito. For two and a half years, until the development of the jet fighter, it was the fastest 'plane in the world. The 425 mph Wooden Wonder was in turn bomber, night and day fighter, photo reconnaissance 'plane and carrier for a six pounder gun. A total of 7,785 were built, more than 3,000 of them at Hatfield, and their contribution to the Allied victory is incalculable.

As the war drew to its close, the development of Frank Whittle's jet engine took De Havilland's into a new age of flight. Major Frank Halford, the company's chief engine designer, produced the Goblin which was used to power the first De Havilland jet, the 531 mph single seat Vampire fighter; 1,157 were built. The Sea Vampire was the first jet to land on an aircraft carrier and the later development, the Venom with its larger Ghost engine, could reach 576 mph at sea level. But peace brought renewed demands for civil aircraft and the prospect of a jet airliner took shape. De Havilland's imagination, skill and enterprise grasped the glittering prize and found both triumph and disaster.

The first step towards the company's — and Britain's — greatest achievement in peacetime flying was stained with personal tragedy for the de Havilland family. The company developed the DH108 Swallow, an experimental tail-less single seat 'plane powered by a Goblin engine. Its speed potential encouraged Geoffrey, the founder's son and then chief test pilot of the company, gradually to increase its performance until he felt he could bid to beat the then world speed record of 616 mph. On 27 September 1946 his father saw him off from Hatfield on another test flight. Over the Thames estuary the Swallow exploded in a dive; Geoffrey's body was washed ashore at Whitstable a few days later. His brother John had died in 1943 in a mid-air collision while test flying a Mosquito. Their father later wrote simply of their deaths: 'Both had died doing the work they loved above all else'. They are buried with their mother in Tewin churchyard.

Geoffrey's death meant the company needed a new chief test pilot. They found him in John Cunningham, a boyish-faced young man who had joined their Training School before the war and had a distinguished military record flying Mosquitoes. Despite his indifference to fame, he was to become one of the best known test pilots in the world.

Work on the DH106 airliner proceeded. Under tight security it was subjected to thousands of hours of tests as the company took flying into a brave new world. On the morning of 27 July 1949 the gleaming silver 'plane made its first public appearance at Hatfield before the world's press and guests including Frank Whittle. On its side was painted the name it had inherited from its dashing predecessor: the Comet.

The morning was an anti-climax. The Comet taxied along the runway and was only airborne for a few moments in a couple of 500 yard hops. In the evening, when the press had gone, it flew for the first time, taking off at 6.17 and staying airborne for 31 minutes, reaching a height of 10,000 feet. John Cunningham was at the controls with John Wilson second pilot, Frank Reynolds flight engineer, Harold 'Tubby' Waters flight engineer (electronics) and Tony Fairbrother flight test observer. By a happy coincidence, it was both Sir Geoffrey's and John Cunningham's birthday.

British Overseas Airways had already placed its first Comet orders. The first, G-ALYP call sign Yoke Peter, flew from London to Johannesburg on 2 May 1952, the first jet passenger service in the world. In the drab, ration-booked Britain of the postwar years, it was a golden moment of national pride. Three weeks after the first BOAC flight, the Queen Mother and Princess Margaret, accompanied by Lord and Lady Salisbury, flew from Hatfield on a four-hour flight across Europe. In the first year of BOAC service, Comets carried 28,000 passengers and flew more than 100 million miles. Hatfield had never had it so good.

Disaster struck savagely twice in 1954. There had been one earlier accident near Calcutta in 1953 when a Comet crashed in a storm with no survivors, but this had been attributed to natural causes. But on 10 January 1954 Yoke Peter — the first Comet in service and the 'plane in which Prince Philip had flown from Hatfield prior to delivery — inexplicably plunged into the Mediterranean near Elba, killing all 35 on board, including six children; 88 days later on 8 April another did the same near Naples. All Comets were grounded and a Court of Inquiry set up.

As well as the shattering effect on the morale of Hatfield, the inevitable cutback in work at the factory had disastrous repercussions. Workers found their earnings severely reduced as overtime was abandoned: one report was of a man whose pay packet dropped from £32 to £7 in a week. Families cancelled their holidays, cars were sold, television sets returned. In the months after the crashes about 1,000 jobs were lost at Hatfield and the Rural District Council expressed concern — somewhat belatedly — that this was a one-industry town. The future hung on the Court of Inquiry.

The remains of Yoke Peter were recovered from the sea bed by ingenious submarine engineering and fully examined. The inquiry, which sat in public, heard 800,000 words of evidence from 68 witnesses on technical theories as to the cause. One completely non-technical comment came from Lord Brabazon, chairman of the Air Registration Board: 'You and I know the cause of this accident. It is due to the adventurous, pioneering spirit of our race'. The findings of the inquiry under Lord Cohen essentially agreed. De Havilland's had taken manned flight beyond new frontiers and, despite the exhaustive, exacting tests the Comet had been put through before going into the air, the then little-known problems of metal fatigue had caused the disasters: one crack in the structure had caused the whole pressurised cabin to tear apart.

With cabin modifications, new models of the Comet continued in production, now with Rolls Royce Avon engines. Orders came in from BOAC, the RAF and foreign airlines. A total of 112 were built, 71 at Hatfield. The last of these was completed in December 1962 although today, more than 15 years later, there are still 19 Comets in operation.

In December 1959 the De Havilland company merged with the Hawker Siddeley Group and the famous family name disappeared from the handsome white buildings on the A1. Sir Geoffrey retired soon after and died in May 1965 aged 73. His ashes were scattered from a De Havilland Trident piloted by John Cunningham over the field in Hampshire where he first flew. The last of the family, Sir Geoffrey's one surviving son Peter, died in January 1977.

Over the years the De Havilland company developed other fields of aeronautics. In 1935 it made Britain's first variable pitch propellers and the company formed from that development eventually linked with two others in 1963 to form Hawker Siddeley Dynamics. As early as 1951, De Havilland Propellers had designed Britain's first operational air-to-air guided missile, Firestreak. Since then it has added Red Top, Martel, Sea Dart and Sky Flash to the deterrent armoury of the West. All have been designed at Hatfield and made at Lostock in Lancashire. For several years the company carried out tests on Britain's ill-fated intercontinental ballistic missile, Blue Streak, which later became the first stage of Europe's space satellite launcher. Its gantry became a familiar landmark by Coopers Green Lane until the project was abandoned in 1962. Today, as well as working on the next generation of missiles, HSD is applying its inherited expertise to other projects, such as propulsion propellers for hovercraft and air conditioning for Concorde and other aircraft.

The 'planes have continued, with the DH classification replaced by HS. As the last of the Comets was being built, Hawker Siddeley Aviation unveiled its successor. On 9 January 1962 John Cunningham took off from Hatfield on the first flight of the Trident airliner. The name had been chosen by the workforce, reflecting the plane's three Rolls Royce Spey engines and tripled-up safety systems. It was the first airliner to have fully automatic landing facilities built in from the design stage; in November 1966 a Trident landed in 50 yards' visibility fog at London when all other aircraft movement was halted. A total of 117 Tridents I, II and III were all built at Hatfield and the 'plane landed a significant export sale when Communist China ordered 35 for its fleet. The first was handed over to the Chinese Ambassador at Hatfield on 13 November 1972.

The highly successful HS125 executive jet first flew from Hatfield in August 1962. Nearly 400 have been sold (1978 price £2 million each), built at Hatfield's sister factory at Chester with Hatfield supplying sales, development and support services. The wings of the European Airbus, the six-nation combination airliner, were designed at Hatfield and won the company the Queen's Award for Technology in 1975; parts are still made here for assembly at Chester.

On 1 January 1978 the Hawker Siddeley company became part of British Aerospace under the Government's nationalisation legislation of the previous year. The early weeks of the new regime were marked with anxiety. With Trident production coming to an end, the company had designed a new 'plane — the HS146 short haul jet airliner — and preliminary factory floor work had begun. But the Hatfield factory was now part of a much larger enterprise and many complex considerations were being weighed in social, financial and political balances before a decision could be taken on whether or not the 146 would in fact go into production. If not, other work from the national aerospace industry could be brought into Hatfield to ensure continued activity, but such a decision would mean that for the first time in more than 40 years Hatfield's 'planemakers would not be producing a new 'plane. It would have seemed unthinkable to Geoffrey de Havilland.

ABOVE: The HS146 short haul jet mock-up in the Hatfield factory.
BELOW: Early days, shortly after De Havilland's arrival in Hatfield.

61

ABOVE LEFT: The de Havilland brothers, Peter, John and Geoffrey, by the tail of a Mosquito, and RIGHT: Sir Geoffrey de Havilland by a Hornet Moth. BELOW: King George VI with De Havilland chairman Alan Butler on a wartime visit to Hatfield.

John Cunningham and the crew after the first Comet flight, and INSET:
Ronald Bishop, designer of the Mosquito and the Comet airliner.

ABOVE: Major Frank Halford, engine designer, Frank Whittle, Sir Geoffrey de Havilland and Charles Walker, chief engineer, at the maiden flight of the Comet. BELOW: The 25th anniversary of the Comet flight. From left: John Wilson, John Cunningham, Frank Reynolds and Tony Fairbrother. The fifth member of the original crew, Harold 'Tubby' Waters, died in a Comet crash in 1953.

64

ABOVE: The Queen Mother and Princess Margaret at Hatfield for their
Comet flight in May 1952. BELOW: After the first Trident flight in
January 1962.

ABOVE: The Blue Streak gantry at Hawker Siddeley Dynamics in October 1961. BELOW LEFT: The Chinese Ambassador steps aboard the first Trident for the People's Republic of China at Hatfield in November 1973. (HA) RIGHT: Sea Dart being fired. (All pictures BA except that of the Chinese Ambassador.)

66

Running in the Family

In the records of the 13th century the name Bassilly or Baseley is found in Hatfield. Today's Bassills or Basills could be direct descendants, although written evidence has not been found; if it ever emerges, 700 years will be bridged. However, from yeoman Symon Bassill in the later 16th century the line of this farming family is distinct, now prosperous, now in decline. John Bassill was one of the first residents of the New Town in 1851 and today's members of the family descend from the marriage of his daughter Elizabeth to her cousin George.

No other family can claim so long an association with the town, but several have been here a considerable time. The Walbys have been Hatfield butchers for 250 years and possibly longer. From 1684 four Williams, variously related, carried on the business in Duck Lane (today's Park Street): we find one paying £190 to Lord Salisbury in 1761 for 160 'fatt sheep'. The fourth William married Martha Tasker but died five years later in 1770, leaving the young widow with three children. She carried on for 25 years, then on her death the business passed to her second son, George, after he paid his elder brother, another William, £350 for it. In 1823 George sold the Park Street property to the Reverend Charles Maslen, who built the Independent Chapel behind the shop and turned the latter into the Manse. The Walby business moved along Park Street to the corner of Arm and Sword Yard next to the Horse and Groom, where it remained for about 100 years before moving onto the Great North Road. The alteration of that road has left it in the new Salisbury Square. But the long line of butcher Walbys, whose graves at St Etheldreda's cover 150 years, may be ending. Since the death of Joe Walby in 1974, his widow Dorothy has continued the business as her kinswoman Martha did two centuries ago, but there may be nobody in the family to succeed her.

In the 1820s, journeyman bricklayer John Tingey came to Hatfield from Buntingford to establish another lengthy family line. His elder son, another John, was a baker who in 1855 was licensee of the Bakers Arms in Back Street (now Church Street), a building which still stands as a private house. The younger son, Jonathan Edmund, took over Dearman's grocery business in the New Town and expanded into furniture as well. One of the latter's sons, John, continued as a grocer while the other, Edmund, went into furnishing, moving that part of the business to Tingey's Corner Shop on the St Albans Road; today it is Texas Discount and was previously owned by White's of Cheltenham. Edmund's sons, Eric and Rex, continued the furniture business, the latter at Potters Bar, and for many years the company used the old Methodist Chapel on French Horn Lane as a store. Meanwhile grocer John's sons carried on that business; Roland died in 1962, Randall is retired and Norman continues in a shop at the Roe Green Centre in South Hatfield.

Two families independently brought the motor trade to Hatfield. James Gray was born in Welwyn, the youngest of 13 children. Apprenticed to a Hertford coachbuilder, he came to Hatfield — where his father had been born — and set up business in the 1880s. From carriages and landaus he moved into motor cars when they first appeared and turned out both horsedrawn and horseless carriages from a thriving workshop on the London Road near the family home, which stood opposite the old Salisbury Square. He died in 1913 and the business was bought in 1945 by the Clark family, who still run it as Gray's. James Gray's daughter Daisy was born in October 1891 and was christened at midnight when three weeks old by the Rector, Lord William Cecil, because the family feared she might die. In 1977 she celebrated her 86th birthday.

In about 1865 Walter Waters took over the long established Bamford family blacksmith's business in Back Street, moving some 30 years later to the site of the old Militia Barracks in Batterdale where his sons, Fred and George, started taking an interest in cars. In those pioneering days their petrol supplies had to be brought in by horse and cart, as the railway companies charged a prohibitive price because of the fire risk. Waters expanded and in 1925 took over the closed-down Hatfield Brewery site where they remained for about 50 years. After the Barnet by-pass opened in 1927, the business moved out there as well, the brothers building the Stonehouse Hotel next to which their garage and showrooms still stand.

The good barley crops from Hertfordshire's soil laid the foundations of a widespread brewing industry and from the 18th century into the present one it dominated Hatfield. The Searancke family owned the Chequers Inn at the bottom of Fore Street by the 1630s and were among publicans who issued trade tokens as local currency. Within 100 years their development of the Hatfield Brewery had made them major landowners and employers; by 1780 they owned half the north side of Fore Street, the whole of the present Salisbury Square, which was the site of their brewery, and other extensive tracts of land. They suffered a spectacular accident in May 1805 when one of their casks, containing enough for 535 barrels, burst to send a £1,000 river of beer cascading down to join the waters of the River Lea. Ten years after this melancholy occurrence Francis Carter Searancke had sold his family's considerable Hatfield holdings, including a number of pubs. This surprising disposal of an apparently flourishing business may have been a shrewd move, for Francis' partner Joseph Biggs, who paid £11,154 for the whole concern, was bankrupt within four years.

The Brewery was bought by Joseph Field and by the time of his death in 1836 it owned 40 pubs and was producing some 7,600 barrels annually. That year John, Morris and Alfred Pryor, sons of a Baldock brewing family, bought it, Alfred later becoming the sole owner. After his death in 1876 his younger son Edward bought it for £29,442 and subsequently, with his brother-in-law Percy Charles Reid, formed Pryor, Reid and Company. They expanded, absorbing neighbouring breweries in Park Street, the New Town and further afield. Hatfield Brewery closed in 1920, causing considerable concern about unemployment in the town, and its 98 pubs were sold to Benskins Watford Brewery, which was subsequently taken over by Ind Coope.

In 1553 Henry Oliver or Glover was ordered by the Manor Court 'not to throw his skins or hides into the common watercourse of Batterdell', indicating an existing tannery in the town. Butcher William Walby bought the known tannery premises in Batterdale in 1724 and rented out the business, thus securing a ready outlet for the skins of slaughtered animals. By the middle of the last century, after various changes of ownership, the tannery had closed, leaving one James Burgess unemployed. He kept the Compasses alehouse in Fore Street for a while and later became a timber merchant in Batterdale, opposite the site of the old tannery. He died 'a worthy man' in 1878 and his son James John carried on as a builder and undertaker. John James, great-grandson of James the founder Burgess, continues the undertaking business today.

Not unexpectedly in a small community, many families became intertwined by marriage. Thus the Hankins, who arrived when William Hankin came to the town in 1807 and started a descent of tailors and drapers, are linked with Simmons, the bakers and caterers, who in turn married in one generation with the Hulks family, the bakers and grocers of Roe Green, and a distant pattern of marital kinship links them all with the Tingeys. A Walby once married a Hankin and the son of that marriage in turn married one of the Canhams, publicans in Hatfield from 1864.

Among several traceable lines of doctors in the town is one of particular interest. It begins in the 17th century with at least two generations of the Longstaff barber surgeons and there is then a possible link with John Heaviside, who took the lease on the former George Inn at the top of Church Street in the 1740s. Some 30 years later he retired and James Penrose took over and in 1793 was appointed Surgeon Extraordinary to George III and Surgeon to His Majesty's Household. The practice passed on to Penrose's nephew, Carr Ellison Lucas, who by the 1820s had taken William Lloyd Thomas into partnership. A founder Fellow of the Royal College of Surgeons, it was Lloyd Thomas who identified what remains could be found of the 1st Marchioness after the Hatfield House fire in 1835.

In 1848 Lloyd Thomas, faced with a smallpox epidemic, was joined by Charles Drage, who later became his partner and married his daughter Elinor Margaret. With a large London practice as well as his Hatfield one, Drage counted four Prime Ministers (Wellington, Melbourne, Palmerston and Salisbury) among his patients, tackled diphtheria with liberal quantities of port wine and had an air of authority that inspired total confidence among those he treated. He continued in practice until 1912 and died ten years later aged 97. His son, who had joined the practice in 1885, died three years before him. Subsequently the practice has been run by Dr Ballance, Dr Lamb, Dr Jamieson, Dr Hutchin and, since 1975, Dr Mark Rathbone.

Since the Saxons coaxed a living out of Hatfield's soil — here fertile, there barren — farming has been a pursuit of many of the town's families. The Bassills, Currells, Crawfords, Battells, Horns, Biggs, Sherriffs and Webbs are among many who followed what was for centuries Hatfield's main activity, until 20th century urban development drastically reduced it. From the 16th to 18th centuries most of the farmed land was arable with crops of wheat, barley and oats and by the middle of the 18th century sheep were being raised on a substantial scale.

The 1st Marchioness of Salisbury took an active part in the farming interests of the Cecil estates and progressively experimented with her stock, feeding cabbage and carrots to cows, parsnips to oxen and lettuce to pigs — who grew to 48 stone on it. Her son, the 2nd Marquess, faced with an outbreak of cattle disease in a neighbouring herd, stood in the middle of the road and turned back cattle from the infected area to protect his own stock. By the early years of this century the pattern had changed and there was more pasture than arable land in the parish, and by the First World War imported mutton from Australia and New Zealand had wrecked the home market, so that the animals are scarcely found in Hatfield today. The farms now surround the town they once dominated, which has turned its attention to less rustic occupations.

ABOVE: Arm and Sword Yard, on the corner of which Walby's butchers stood for nearly a century. CENTRE: Hatfield 17th century trade tokens. BELOW: The double wedding of Martha and Rachel Burgess, daughters of James Burgess, in 1897. Between them sits Rachel, third wife and widow of James Burgess. She attended his first marriage when she was a baby.

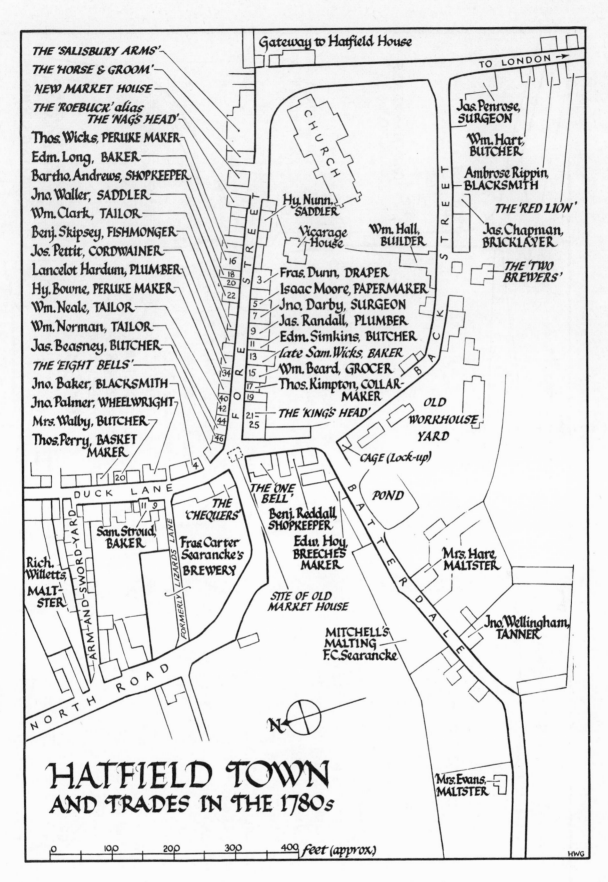

THE 'SALISBURY ARMS'
THE 'HORSE & GROOM'
NEW MARKET HOUSE
THE 'ROEBUCK' alias THE 'NAGS HEAD'
Thos. Wicks, PERUKE MAKER
Edm. Long, BAKER
Bartho. Andrews, SHOPKEEPER
Jno. Waller, SADDLER
Wm. Clark, TAILOR
Benj. Skipsey, FISHMONGER
Jos. Pettit, CORDWAINER
Lancelot Hardum, PLUMBER
Hy. Bowne, PERUKE MAKER
Wm. Neale, TAILOR
Wm. Norman, TAILOR
Jas. Beasney, BUTCHER
THE 'EIGHT BELLS'
Jno. Baker, BLACKSMITH
Jno. Palmer, WHEELWRIGHT
Mrs. Walby, BUTCHER
Thos. Perry, BASKET MAKER

Gateway to Hatfield House
TO LONDON →
CHURCH
Hy. Nunn, SADDLER
Vicarage House
Wm. Hall, BUILDER
FORE STREET
BACK STREET
Jas. Penrose, SURGEON
Wm. Hart, BUTCHER
Ambrose Rippin, BLACKSMITH
THE 'RED LION'
Jas. Chapman, BRICKLAYER
THE 'TWO BREWERS'

16
18
20
22
3
Fras. Dunn, DRAPER
Isaac Moore, PAPERMAKER
5
Jno. Darby, SURGEON
7
Jas. Randall, PLUMBER
9
Edm. Simkins, BUTCHER
11
13
late Sam. Wicks, BAKER
15
Wm. Beard, GROCER
17
Thos. Kimpton, COLLAR-MAKER
34
40
42
44
46
19
21
25
THE 'KING'S HEAD'

OLD WORKHOUSE YARD
CAGE (Lock-up)
POND

20
4
DUCK LANE
11 9
THE 'CHEQUERS'
THE 'ONE BELL'
Benj. Reddall, SHOPKEEPER
Edw. Hoy, BREECHES MAKER
Sam. Stroud, BAKER
Fras Carter Searancke's BREWERY
ARM-AND-SWORD YARD
FORMERLY LIZARDS LANE
Rich. Willetts, MALTSTER
SITE OF OLD MARKET HOUSE
MITCHELL'S MALTING F.C.Searancke
BATTERDALE
Mrs. Hare MALTSTER
Jno. Wellingham, TANNER

NORTH ROAD

N

Mrs. Evans, MALTSTER

HATFIELD TOWN
AND TRADES IN THE 1780s

0   100   200   300   400 feet (approx.)

HWG

1780s map from *Hatfield and its People*, drawn by Henry Gray.

71

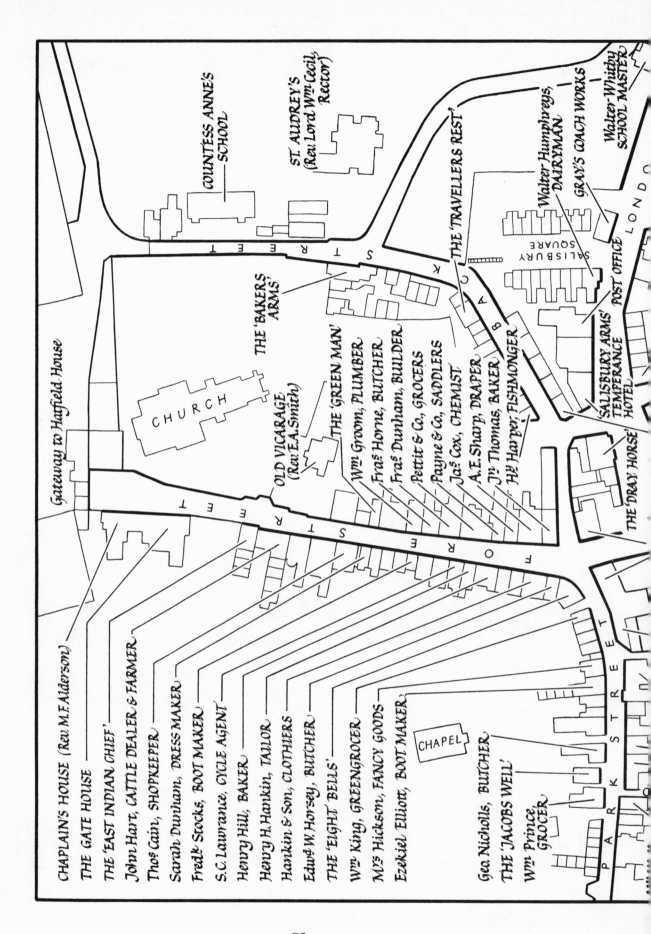

CHAPLAIN'S HOUSE (Rev. M.F. Alderson)

THE GATE HOUSE

THE 'EAST INDIAN CHIEF'

John Hart, CATTLE DEALER & FARMER

Thos. Cain, SHOPKEEPER

Sarah Dunham, DRESS MAKER

Fredk. Stocks, BOOT MAKER

S.C. Lawrance, CYCLE AGENT

Henry Hill, BAKER

Henry H. Hankin, TAILOR

Hankin & Son, CLOTHIERS

Edwd. W. Horsey, BUTCHER

THE 'EIGHT BELLS'

Wm. King, GREENGROCER

Mrs. Hickson, FANCY GOODS

Ezekiel Elliott, BOOT MAKER

Geo. Nicholls, BUTCHER

THE 'JACOBS WELL'

Wm. Prince, GROCER

Gateway to Hayfield House

CHURCH

OLD VICARAGE (Rev. E.A. Smith)

THE 'GREEN MAN'

Wm. Groom, PLUMBER

Fras. Horne, BUTCHER

Fras. Dunham, BUILDER

Pettit & Co., GROCERS

Payne & Co., SADDLERS

Jas. Cox, CHEMIST

A.E. Sharp, DRAPER

Jn. Thomas, BAKER

Hy. Harper, FISHMONGER

THE 'BAKERS ARMS'

COUNTESS ANNE'S SCHOOL

ST. AUDREY'S (Rev. Lord Wm. Cecil, Rector)

THE 'TRAVELLERS REST'

Walter Humphreys, DAIRYMAN

GRAY'S COACH WORKS

Walter Whitby, SCHOOL MASTER

SALISBURY SQUARE

POST OFFICE

SALISBURY ARMS' TEMPERANCE HOTEL

THE 'DRAY HORSE'

CHAPEL

STREET

FORE STREET

BAT

LONDO

PARK STREET

72

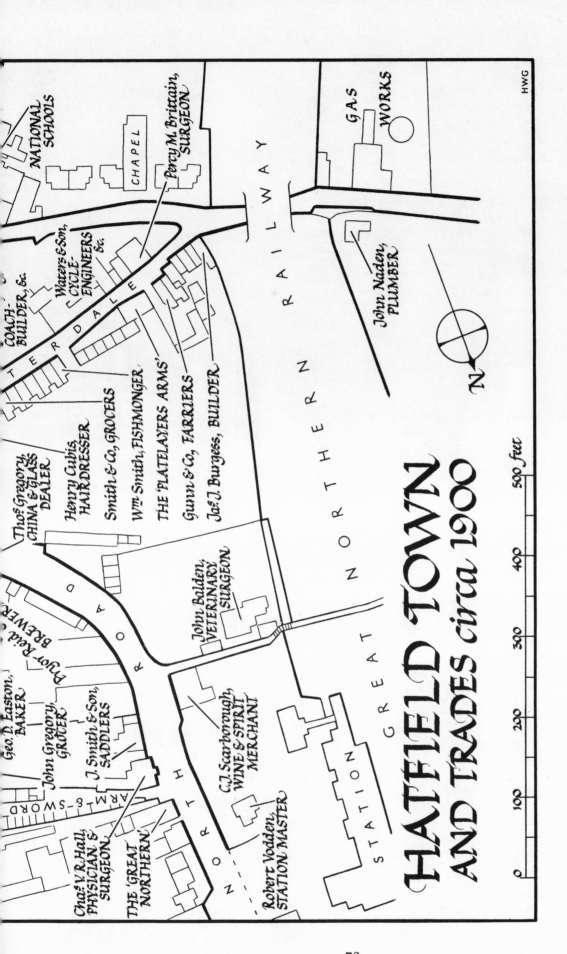

HATFIELD TOWN AND TRADES circa 1900

NATIONAL SCHOOLS

CHAPEL

Percy M. Brittain, SURGEON

COACH-BUILDER, &c.

Waters & Son, CYCLE-ENGINEERS, &c.

Thos Gregory, CHINA & GLASS DEALER

Henry Cubis, HAIRDRESSER

Smith & Co, GROCERS

Wm Smith, FISHMONGER

THE 'PLATELAYERS ARMS'

Gunn & Co, FARRIERS

Jas J. Burgess, BUILDER

RAILWAY

GAS WORKS

John Naden, PLUMBER

GREAT NORTHERN RAILWAY

Pryor Reid BREWERY

Geo D. Easton, BAKER

John Gregory, GROCER

J. Smith & Son, SADDLERS

Chas V.R. Hall, PHYSICIAN & SURGEON

THE 'GREAT NORTHERN'

Robert Vodden, STATION MASTER

C.J. Scarborough, WINE & SPIRIT MERCHANT

John Balden, VETERINARY SURGEON

STATION

N

500 feet

0 100 200 300 400 500

HWG

1900 map specially drawn for this book by Henry Gray.

ABOVE: James Gray, left, with his workers outside their Great North
Road premises, (JH) and INSET: Daisy Gray, daughter of James, aged 86.
BELOW: Gray's business card.

ABOVE: Batterdale in 1965. (CNT) BELOW: Workers on the Hatfield
estate earlier this century. (JH)

ABOVE: The Tingey grocery shop on St Albans Road in the 1920s. (RT)
BELOW: John Tingey (on cart) and Albert Rumney in Fench Horn Lane
before 1914. (RT)

76

ABOVE: The Stonehouse: an original drawing by Roger Eaton. BELOW: Roe Green farm, demolished in 1966. There had been a farm there since the 13th century. (CNT)

ABOVE and CENTRE: Two views of Park Street around the turn of the century. BELOW: William Hulks, Hatfield New Town baker, in the early years of this century. (JH)

ABOVE: Fore Street in 1904. BELOW: Harvest time at Roe Green during
the First World War. (JH)

ABOVE: Filling in the brewery cellars during the building of Salisbury
Square. (JF) BELOW: Inside Hatfield Brewery yard, 1967. (CNT)

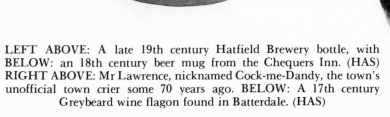

LEFT ABOVE: A late 19th century Hatfield Brewery bottle, with BELOW: an 18th century beer mug from the Chequers Inn. (HAS) RIGHT ABOVE: Mr Lawrence, nicknamed Cock-me-Dandy, the town's unofficial town crier some 70 years ago. BELOW: A 17th century Greybeard wine flagon found in Batterdale. (HAS)

ABOVE: Cage Hill at the bottom of Church Street. The shop was the site
of a local lock-up for lawbreakers. BELOW: The Board of Guardians of
the former Hatfield Workhouse, 1930.

82

Power of Assembly

By the charters of six kings Hugh Balsam, Bishop of Ely in 1278, claimed absolute powers of law and order over those of his manor at Hatfield. He could possess the goods of a convicted felon or fugitive and have the use of his land for a year and a day; he could try any offence and impose appropriate punishments from the ducking stool to the gallows; the children of his villeins were his property. There are no records of how strictly he enforced these draconian powers.

One of the earliest recorded lawbreakers in Hatfield was John Wykinge who, on 14 September 1391, was fined sixpence by the Manor Court at Symondshyde for damaging a fishpond with his horse. The same court ruled that 'Joan, daughter of John Potter, is beyond the domain without licence of the lord; she is to re-enter the domain under a penalty of twenty shillings'. From these distant figures, there tumbles down the centuries a varied collection of mischiefs and villains, petty and serious, in a pattern of crime and punishment familiar throughout England.

In 1482 John and James Turner were fined fourpence each for making bad quality shoes; William Walker was fined twopence in 1505 for selling his meat at too high a price and nearly half a century later, now accompanied by his son, was making regular appearances for the same offence. In 1534 Sir Thomas More was fined fourpence for not attending court as a landowner in the parish, with land at Down's Farm; as he was within a year of his execution by Henry VIII, Sir Thomas had more pressing matters to concern him. Stephen Care was fined twenty pence in 1553 because he 'frequents immoderately houses where ale is sold and rarely goes to church'; among the keepers of unlicensed alehouses in 1656 was a Hatfield labourer with a memorable name — William Shakespaire. In 1690 John Manlove stole fruit from Lord Salisbury and was whipped for an hour on Market Day, tied to the end of a cart pulling him up and down the street; some 70 years later sawyer Richard Greenham and tripeman William Bibby were transported for seven long years for stealing £2 worth of poultry; in 1870 labourers George Young and Daniel Shuffle were transported for life for stealing a sheep.

Out of this background of everyday offences, which continues at the Monday sittings of Hatfield magistrates today, there emerge the more sinister, notorious or bizarre. In 1593 spinster Joan Garret appeared before Hertford Assize charged with witchcraft. Her Hatfield neighbours alleged she had been busy between 1586 and 1592, when she had bewitched four different people, all of whom 'languished and then died'. And she had bewitched William Marshall's horse for good measure. The fact that one victim spent five years languishing must have influenced the jury, for they found her guilty only of enchanting the horse and she was jailed for a year. Her contemporary, labourer George Webb, was less fortunate. Charged with stealing £1 1s 4d worth of household linen, he claimed benefit of clergy, a device used by many convicted thieves to escape the gallows by proving that they could read. But Webb was unable to make good his claim and was hanged.

The year 1602 produced a bloody and curious murder. A gang killed Essex yeoman Anthony James and his wife and brought their children, Anthony and Elizabeth, to Hatfield. That night baker George Dell cut the boy's throat and threw his body in a pond; Elizabeth had her tongue cut out and was turned loose in Hatfield Wood. Three years later she returned to Hatfield and her distress at seeing Dell again led to inquiries, after which he and Agnes Dell, a widow, possibly his mother, were arrested. There followed the only known Hatfield miracle: the tongueless Elizabeth suddenly began to speak and told the whole story. The understandably suspicious Justices had her confronted by a man dressed as the Devil who threatened to tear her to pieces for lying. Said the bold Elizabeth: 'Good Gaffer Devil, do not hurt me. I speak nothing but truth, and what the thing within me instructeth me to speak.' In 1606 George and Agnes Dell were hanged.

In 1650 the people of Hatfield had an environmental problem because of the activities of Samuel Nicholas, John Miller and William Selwood, who were making potash by burning 'straw steeped in uryne or stale and other filthy waters'. All three were bound over to stop this 'very unwholesome and pestiferous' pursuit. The innocent business of carrying dung landed labourer Robert Prior in trouble in 1662 because he did it on a Sunday. And on 1 August 1694 John Dill was married at St Etheldreda's; he then married another woman at Hertford a month later. The jury found they could not prove the case and left him to sort out his family problems.

In 1733, the year that London sugar refiner Thomas Lewis was robbed between Welwyn and Hatfield as he rode the London Coach by 'a single highwayman in a dark coloured coat', William Harrow, the son of a bricklayer, was born in Hatfield, destined or doomed to become the Flying Highwayman. 'Fond of Company, Cock-Fighting, Horseracing and other Diversions', he turned to crime and after escaping from Hertford jail, formed a gang which terrorised the county. After robbing farmer Thomas Glasscock of £300 (of which he hid two thirds for himself from the rest of the gang) he fled to the Midlands and was arrested in bed with his mistress in Worcester. Condemned to hang at Hertford, he wrenched himself free of his chains the night before his execution, but this time was unable to find a way out of his cell. Faced with the inevitable, he 'gave a violent Spring' on the rope's end and finished it off quickly.

Sarah Packer, a lively troublemaker, spent the 1770s assaulting her neighbours and being regularly whipped or imprisoned, and in 1790 the Hertford Prison Records show payment of seven shillings to convey Elizabeth Gelding to Hatfield and five shillings to whip her. But that same year brought a case of particular social significance.

Thomas Vallance was a papermaker with a mill at Mill Green. In 1790 eleven of his employees demanded a pay increase of a shilling a week; if this was not agreed within 14 days they would leave his employment. Such action was intolerable (within ten years Pitt's Combination Act banning Trade Unions was to be passed) and all the men were found guilty of conspiracy 'with force and arms'. What happened to them is not known; the name of one, John Wade, appears twice in the prison records, once as having died a natural death and again as having been hanged. Vallance continued in business.

The good order of the town involved all the administrative activities, including the care of the poor. The Cecil family accounts for 1619 show £21 shared between 111 old people, among them the unfortunate William Keating, 'he being forgotten the last yeare'. Each parish was responsible for its own poor and there was constant bickering as to where the

84

responsibility lay. In 1631 Hatfield successfully petitioned for Totteridge — said to have wealthy inhabitants and few poor — to be included in its parish and pay towards the cost. The row with Totteridge, which naturally objected to this arrangement, was still flourishing years later, and in the spring of 1684 the people of Hatfield protested that William Willson, his wife and four children had been imposed on them after being arrested as vagrants at Hertford. Willson had lived in the town some ten years previously but, claimed the townsfolk, had left a single man. Who, they demanded, was this woman, adding darkly that they suspected he had never been lawfully married. Their case was simple: either the unfortunate Willson produced a marriage certificate or the woman must go. As for the children, let those parishes where they had been born have care of them; Hatfield had enough on its collective plate.

But few took such a firm hold of this thorny problem as James, 2nd Marquess of Salisbury, who obtained dictatorial powers over parish matters in return for guaranteeing that the Poor Rate would not exceed five shillings in the pound. Finding the workhouse filthy, its inmates unemployed and money paid out for pretended illnesses being spent in the alehouse, the firm but not unenlightened Marquess put things in order. He appointed a committee — whose decisions he could ignore — and sought a permanent workhouse overseer, 'preferably a man accustomed to military discipline'. The workhouse was extended to accommodate 130 and two rooms were set aside for a hospital. Every man going to work was given 1½ lbs of bread and ¼ lb of cheese for breakfast and dinner with a hot meal at night; women received ¾lb bread a day, an ounce of tea and ½lb of butter and sugar a week; children were given milk pottage for breakfast and bread and cheese for dinner. Everyone received six ounces of cooked meat with vegetables three times a week for supper and on other days broth thickened with rice 'and without limitation'. Wrote the Marquess to an acquaintance in 1827: 'Some parts of the dietary may appear luxurious, but, the privation of it as a punishment is sufficiently great to preserve the best discipline amongst them'. While the men worked on the roads, the women cooked, brewed, baked and washed and the children wound silk; those too young to work were taught to read and write. The average weekly cost for each inmate was 2s 11¾d.

For the idle and feckless, the stern Marquess had no sympathy. Anyone unemployable because of bad character should be given 'an occupation which, by the ridicule attaching to it, would be most particularly irksome to his feelings and have the effect of deterring others from the same conduct'. One suggestion was to make the reprobate dig a hole for the sake of filling it up again — a true Army influence. If the man refused such work he was jailed.

The Marquess's system of dealing with beggars drew praise from many. Householders were issued with tickets which they gave to the beggar at the door; he could take it to the workhouse and obtain a free meal on condition that he stayed the night and was subjected to the usual disciplines, including being washed and put to work if he was able. Most of them refused the deal and walked off, to be speedily arrested by the parish constable if they begged again.

Accustomed to running matters his own way, the Marquess strenuously opposed the formation of a county police force under the Rural Police Act. When the Court of Quarter Sessions met in 1841 to appoint a Chief Constable, he objected to the election and only lost the argument by a single vote. He then simply said the whole proceeding was illegal. Some years later in 1856 he seems to have accepted the system and contributed towards a gold snuff box and 20 guineas presented to Inspector Abraham English, who had successfully captured arsonists in Hatfield.

The contentious Local Government Act of 1894 brought Hatfield within a national framework of local administration. For centuries the town had been content to have its affairs run by the various Manor Lords, the Church or the powerful Cecils; now the first elections were to be held for Rural District and Parish Councils and the Parish Meeting. The first Parish Meeting was held in December 1894 and both that body and the Parish Council continue today, the council being one of the largest of its kind in England, with a budget of more than £100,000 in 1977-78, and one of the few with a full-time Clerk. The Rural Council first met in January 1895 and continued until further local government reshaping in 1974 when it held its last meeting in the Old Palace before becoming part of the new Welwyn Hatfield District Council. Meanwhile the New Towns Act of 1948 had designated Hatfield a New Town and this development of the modern town became part of the work of the Commission for the New Towns.

Hatfield's market days stretch back to 1226 when Henry III granted the Bishops of Ely the rights to an annual four-day fair and a Thursday market. Standing on 12 timber stilts, the Market House was originally at the bottom of Fore Street, but was later moved to the top, opposite the church. Near the site there remains a brick circle in the ground which was used as a cattle auction ring. The church connection with the fairs held on the feast of St Etheldreda added a word to the language; Etheldreda became Aldreda in Latin and was converted back to English as Audrey. Thus St Audrey became garbled into 'tawdry' and the new-coined adjective described the indifferent goods on sale; this happened in other places which had a connection with the saint. The Hatfield market was an important one and in 1682 Lord Salisbury granted William Wright the profitable business of setting up the stalls and pens. Wright complained he was losing money because local residents traditionally set up stalls outside their homes for tradespeople and thus undermined his hoped-for monopoly. The annual fair lasted into this century, but by 1888 the market had vanished and was not re-established until 1957 in the New Town.

Hatfield constabulary about 1880.

86

ABOVE: Hatfield Fire Brigade dressed as Gold Rush prospectors about 1900, and BELOW: more conventionally attired in the 1930s. INSET: Hatfield fire station in Batterdale.

LEFT ABOVE: The Ma
Street, drawn by J. C.
CENTRE: seen from t
Hatfield market in the
ABOVE: Hatfield Rura
(JF) BELOW CENTRE
L. Burvill-Holmes outs
years, in March 1967,
last meeting of Hatfield
March

e at the top of Fore
1832, (CRO) and
in 1847. BELOW:
in 1978. RIGHT
Council, 1969-70,
RDC chairman Dr
t, his home for 40
and RIGHT: the
e Old Palace on 27
HT)

Mr J. Lloyd
and the clerk

The clerk reported, that the following cheques
have been signed since the last Meeting of the
Trustees:

Eliz.ᵗʰ Humphreys ½ yrs annuity to Mids: 1885 £5.0.0
Sarah Dunham   "   "   "   5.0.0
Sarah Webb   "   "   "   5.0.0
Lucy M. Cannon   "   "   "   5.0.0
Revd J. Thompson, for the late Jane Hammond }
   77 days, annuity to 15ᵗ March 1885 ——   } 2.2.6
Catherine Orme, 104 days, annuity from 18ᵗ }
        March /85 to Mids: /85 ——   } 2.17.6
The Clerk, Salary ½ yr. to Mids: /85 —— £2.10.0
          Stationery, Stamps &c ——   3.6
                                      2.13.6
Sarah Dunham, ½ yrs, annuity to Xmas 1885 5.0.0
Sarah Webb   "   "   "   5.0.0

ABOVE: An extract from the 1885 records of the Sir Francis Boteler
Charity, which dates from 1694 and still pays an annual sum of money to
four Hatfield widows and one from Tewin. BELOW: Burgomeister Theo
de Meester of Zierikzee, Hatfield's twin town since 1954 (second right),
with his wife, Parish Council chairman 'Bunny' Rogers (second left) and
District Council chairman Bill Storey.

Under Instruction

In 1596 Robert Cloughe was granted a licence to teach in Hatfield by the Bishop of London, the earliest incomplete evidence of formal education in the town. Thereafter education, the privilege of the rich, is absent from the records until 1732 when Anne, widow of the undistinguished 5th Earl of Salisbury, founded her charity school, with an eye to ensuring a steady supply of girls equipped for domestic service as much as to improving the minds of the deserving poor. The original intention was 'to teach in the School 20 poor girls, children of the poor inhabitants in the Parish of Hatfield, to read and . . . to do other useful and necessary things in order to fit them for services and other employments and also to instruct them in the principles of the Christian religion'. There was £10 to provide each girl with a gown and coat of cheap brown cloth with a cap, band, gloves, stays, apron, stockings and shoes; the uniform had to last for two years. The Countess Anne School originally stood near today's Lawn House, moved to the lodge at the top of Fore Street and in the 1870s went into the building on Church Street — now the church hall — which was used as a temporary place of worship while St Etheldreda's was being restored. The school closed in its 180th year in 1912, but the name persisted. The pupils of today's Countess Anne School in School Lane can still see the immense sampler dating from 1735 which lists the nine simple but strict orders which the disciplinarian Countess expected the first grateful pupils to obey absolutely.

Following Countess Anne's example, a long line of private schools, of varying educational quality, appeared in the town. Most came and went without anyone recording a comment on them, but the Reverend Thomas Ray, an independent Minister who ran a boarding school in Fore Street for 17 boys in the middle of the last century, achieved his little immortality when a nine-year-old pupil, visiting his uncle in the town, attended for a few weeks. The boy was the young Thomas Hardy and the novelist later recalled Mr Ray's school as being 'somewhat on the Squeers's model'; perhaps Mr Ray would rather have remained anonymous.

The private school run by the Rector, the Reverend Francis Faithfull, had Lord Robert Cecil, later the 3rd Marquess of Salisbury, as a pupil. Sadly, Lord Robert's schooldays were among the unhappiest of his life and he recalled his period there with acute misery. In 1852 the 2nd Marquess had become embroiled in the education question, writing to Faithfull with his customary forthrightness. The schools in the parish were run 'rather to the benefit of the schoolmaster than the scholar', he complains, and 'no attempt is made to render education agreeable. It is all work, nothing interesting'. The solution, he suggests, would be to teach children skills that would be useful in later life as well as giving them formal education, and there should be evening classes for boys at work 'and many valuable members of society would be produced'.

Out of the irregular pattern of private schools there eventually emerged a national,

Government supported system. The National Society for Promoting the Education of the Poor in the Principles of the Established Church set up the first National School in Hatfield with State support in the 1830s. The classroom was probably above the Market House, which then stood at the top of Fore Street opposite St Etheldreda's. In 1850 the 2nd Marquess and Rector Faithfull were among the principal founders of the London Road School, which stood near the site of Gray's garage today. The original bill for setting up the school is added up incorrectly (it should be £715 18s, not £713 10s) — silent but eloquent testimony to the need for better education. By the end of the 19th century, its numbers increased by compulsory school attendance, the redbrick building was too small for its population and in 1905 a new school opened in Endymion Road. The pupils were dispersed among the new building, the London Road School and the Countess Anne premises after they became available in 1912. By the 1920s the London Road School, out of date and unhygienic, had closed and in October 1944 the Endymion Road school, by then called St Audrey's, was destroyed by a flying bomb. A new school was built on the site and after St Audrey's moved to Travellers Lane in 1957, the building was the temporary home of Broad Oaks Junior and Onslow Schools while their premises were being built. Later it took the name of the Countess Anne School.

A lending library to improve the adult mind was opened in Hatfield in 1855; five years later it had some 4,200 books. By 1978 the Hatfield County Library in Queensway had about 48,000 volumes on its shelves. In 1865 there were weekly Penny Readings in the town for the entertainment and enlightenment of the people. On one occasion the Reverend C. J. Robinson diverted his audience with a reading of the death of Dickens' Little Nell 'somewhat heavily perhaps, but most pathetically and with a solemnity becoming the sacredness of the subject', as a newspaper report observed.

The biggest educational project in Hatfield began in 1946 when Alan S. Butler, then chairman of the De Havilland Aircraft Company, gave 90 acres of land to the county council on condition that it should be used for education. It became the site of one of three technical colleges in the county.

Officially opened by the Duke of Edinburgh on 16 December 1952, the college had started teaching its first students the previous September. The first year's intake totalled 1,700 and by its silver jubilee in 1977 what had become Hatfield Polytechnic had 4,000 students, more than half of them full-time, and its own computer.

The Fore Street Lodge, sometime home of Countess Anne School, drawn by Beresford Johnson.

ABOVE: The sampler that hangs in the present Countess Anne School, listing the 'Orders To be observed in this Charity School as given by the Right Honourable Anne, Countess of Salisbury, the 29 day of September 1735: I The 20 Girls be Taught on the Foundation to Read, Sew, Knit and Mark in order to Fit them for Services: And the School to consist of Forty Girls only. II That an exact List of their Names be kept and called over every Day. III That none be admitted under Nine nor continued after Fifteen years of age. IV That if any of the Charity-Children are absent from School three days in one Month (times of Breaking up, a Month in Harvest and Sicknefs excepted) to be Expelled. Also in case they are guilty of Swearing, Pilfering, or any other disorderly Behaviour, as well out of School as in School; and likewise if they are not kept Neat and Clean. V That Prayers be read every Morning and Afternoon with the Psalms and Lefsons appointed for the Day. VI That the Children continue at School in Summer from Seven o'Clock to Twelve in the Morning, And from Two to Five in the Afternoon: And in Winter from Eight to Twelve in the Morning and One to Four in the Afternoon. VII That two Lefsons be said in the Morning and Two in the Afternoon. VIII That all Days be alike except Thursdays and Saturdays to One o'Clock in the Afternoon: And that on those Days the Explanation of the Church-Catechism or Foxes Publick Worship be Taught weekly. And whereas many have abused the Charitable Dispofition of the said Countefs of Salisbury by taking their Children out of the School before they were qualified as aforesaid for Services contrary to her Ladiships Charity and good intentions, it is therefore most strictly to be observed, IX That whoever take their Child or Children out of the School without the Consent and Approbation of the said Countefs of Salisbury, neither Themselves nor their Children shall for the Future partake of her Ladiship's Bounty in any kind whatsoever.'

Lady Anne Tufton, 5th Countess of Salisbury. (MoS)

ABOVE: St Audrey's pupils about 1912 with teacher Miss Ellingham.
(AL) BELOW: St Audrey's circa 1915 with teacher Mr Bottomley. (AL)

94

Expences.

The Building itself   £530 . 13 . 8.
Furnishing Schools Galleries &c   64 . 18 . 6
Furnishing Teacher's Residence   27 . 6 . 3.
Outworks   25 . 1 . 10.
Architect   47 . 17 . 9 .
Clerk of the Works   20 . 0 . 0.
                 £ 713 . 10 . 0.

ABOVE: The London Road School. BELOW LEFT: The bell from the school at today's St Audrey's in Travellers Lane. RIGHT: The incorrectly added-up bill for the London Road School.

95

ABOVE: Footballers from Dagmar House School, one of the private schools in Hatfield in the 1920s. Principal John Sheehan-Dare is on the left. (RT) BELOW: Children from Countess Anne School rehearsing for a folk dancing pageant in Hatfield Park in June 1936.

96

ABOVE: Goldings school, a private kindergarten, in 1953 with Miss Norman, who ran it, on the right. (RT) BELOW: The Duke of Edinburgh at the opening of Hatfield Technical College in December 1952. On his right is the Principal, Dr William Chapman.

ABOVE: Lively times with the South Herts Yeomanry. (HYAHT)
BELOW: 'Mother', the original tank, in Hatfield Park for its trials.
(RACTM)

98

Musket, Fife and Drum

Neither battle, skirmish nor military scuffle has been fought in Hatfield, but for nearly two centuries there were soldiers based in the town. The Militia Act of 1757 made the scarlet coats with old gold facings a familiar sight and Hatfield was the headquarters of the Hertfordshire Militia from 1853 until they moved to Hertford 20 years later. The local forces were long connected with the Cecil family. The 1st Marquess had absolute responsibility for raising the Militia (by ballot of able-bodied men) after he became Lord Lieutenant of the county in 1771, a position he held for more than 50 years. The 2nd Marquess was Colonel of the Militia from 1815 to his death in 1868 and the 4th Marquess commanded the Militia as Lord Cranborne when they won their first battle honour in South Africa in 1900-02. The only surviving Militia colours hang in St Etheldreda's and the church also has a memorial to J. S. Collings-Wells, who was killed commanding the 4th Battalion Bedfordshire Regiment, as the Militia had become, during the March Retreat of 1918. He was posthumously awarded the Victoria Cross.

The Hertfordshire Yeomanry Cavalry were first raised in 1794, but had no direct connection with the town. In 1830 they were re-raised as the South Hertfordshire Yeomanry Cavalry with their headquarters at Hatfield under the command of the 2nd Marquess. He resigned in 1853 and 40 years later the Hertfordshire Yeomanry Cavalry, as it had been renamed, ceased its connection with the town, although it has a continuous line of existence to the present day. An infantry company was raised in the town in Napoleonic times, later stood down and then reformed as part of the 1st Regiment Hertfordshire Volunteer Infantry in 1803, but was disbanded five years later when the threat from France was judged to have subsided.

These early military activities were part of a national pattern and have left no impression on today's Hatfield. The Militia barracks in Batterdale and the houses in the original Salisbury Square, below Church Street, which were the homes of the permanent staff, have now disappeared, as has the 'Colonel's House' in Batterdale. This latter name is curious. Built in the late 17th century as the home of the prosperous maltster Samuel Hare, the house was used by the Militia Quartermaster, not the Colonel, who was Lord Salisbury and would obviously have no need of it. Nonetheless, the name persisted up to the time of its demolition in the 1960s as part of the Old Town redevelopment.

But the military connection brought one regular entertainment and the most spectacular parade Hatfield has ever witnessed. The regular events were Yeomanry races, which were frequently held in Hatfield Park. These lively affairs attracted large crowds, offered golden opportunities for pickpockets and provided additional amusements such as that noted by a newspaper report in 1860: 'An ugly little Ethiopian sang negro songs and a perfectly hideous and meagre old woman . . . danced on the greensward.'

The great spectacle was in June 1800 when the 1st Marquess organised a Review of troops for King George III. More than 1,400 Militia, Yeomanry Cavalry and men of the

Volunteer Associations marched past their king, their uniforms like massed flowers about the summer grass. The entertainment and refreshments were on a suitably massive scale: 959 beer jugs, 2,670 plates, 538 mustards, salts and cruets, 48 butter boats. Four Hatfield butchers — Simkins, Beasney, Hart and Walby — supplied £150 worth of meat, which was only a small part of the meal. The splendour of the scene was captured by artist Richard Livesay, whose immense oil painting of the parading troops hangs in Hatfield House; a print of the picture is the front endpaper of this book. In the foreground is the figure of John Whitemore listening to a man explaining what is happening. Whitemore is leaning on a stick, understandably as the following year he was to die at the impressive age of 103. The artist and his family are in the left foreground.

In the First World War Hatfield provided 4 Company 3rd Battalion Hertfordshire Volunteer Regiment — a force equivalent to the Home Guard a generation later — and the town gave of its sons in the carnage, the best remembered being the three sons of Rector Lord William Cecil. All were killed in action: Rupert at Ypres in July 1915, Randle at Masnieres in December 1917 and John at Mery in August 1918. A stained glass window in St Etheldreda's perpetuates their memory and their names accompany those of 138 other victims of the Great War on the town's memorial.

But far from the battlefields and wrapped in the closest secrecy, an event of great military significance took place in Hatfield Park in 1916. At 9.15 on the morning of Saturday 29 January, watched only by senior Army and Navy personnel, a 31-foot steel lozenge-shaped box, its sides studded with rivets, rumbled no faster than a man can walk around a special course. Two moveable six-pounder guns protruded from its sides as it crossed trenches and climbed concrete parapets. A few days later, on 2 February, this time watched by Secretary of State for War Field Marshal Earl Kitchener, Minister for Munitions David Lloyd-George and First Lord of the Admiralty Arthur Balfour, it successfully repeated these manoeuvres. These historic occasions were the first official trials of a new engine of war, the tank. That pioneering prototype, appropriately called Mother, was scrapped in 1939, but from 1919 one of its contemporaries stood in Hatfield Park, a gift from Winston Churchill to Lord Salisbury for the use of his land for the trials. It is now in the Royal Armoured Corps Tank Museum near Wareham in Dorset.

The Second World War saw the first victims of hostilities actually in the town. On 3 October 1940, four bombs from a Junkers 88 hit the '94 shop' at De Havilland's, where work was proceeding on the Mosquito. Twenty one people died and a further 70 were injured. Then on 22 September and 10 October 1944, two V1 Flying Bombs hit the town, the first in Selwyn Crescent and the second on St Audrey's School in Endymion Road. In all there were 34 civilian names to be added to the 58 service men and women on the war memorial.

Of the 20 original Home Guard companies raised in the county in 1940, Hatfield provided 10 Company and De Havilland's 19 Company. Soon afterwards, the companies were organised into battalions; 10 Company became part of the 4th Hertfordshire Battalion with 19 Company attached. In July 1942 19 Company achieved battalion status and in September of the same year the Hatfield and Brookmans Park elements of the 4th Battalion were split off to form 14th Hertfordshire Battalion with headquarters at Hatfield. There were also two independent Home Guard anti-aircraft troops at the De Havilland factory, one of which is credited with the destruction of an enemy plane.

The disbanding of the Home Guard saw the end of a long history of soldiering in Hatfield. Those lone surviving Militia colours in St Etheldreda's are all that now remain to show for it.

ABOVE: The 'Colonel's House' in Batterdale. (JFL) BELOW: Salisbury
Square, where the Militia staff was quartered. (CNT)

101

ABOVE: Hatfield Volunteer Training Corps on field exercises in 1915. (HYAHT) BELOW LEFT: Memorial window in St Etheldreda's to the three sons of Lord William Cecil, and RIGHT: the cemetery on the Great North Road for 21 servicemen who died in Hatfield House while it was a military hospital.

ABOVE: Workers from Waters Garage in the First World War when they were making shell cases. (EP) BELOW: Hatfield House as a Second World War military hospital. (MoS)

ABOVE LEFT: Flying bomb damage in Selwyn Crescent, (HA) and RIGHT: Primrose Cottages after a flying bomb hit St Audrey's school opposite. (HA) CENTRE: Effective obstacles to stop enemy aircraft landing at De Havillands. (BA) BELOW LEFT: The first Mosquito just before its maiden flight in 1940, (BA) and RIGHT: a Home Guard parade at De Havilland's, 1942. (BA)

The 1st Marchioness of Salisbury at archery. (CRO)

Pleasurable Pursuits

The scene beneath the April sky of 1557 was dazzling. The slender, russet-haired, 23-year-old Elizabeth Tudor rode out from the Palace at Hatfield followed by twelve attendant ladies in shining white satin and twenty men in bright green. They rode to Enfield Chase where a glittering company of archers, scarlet booted and yellow capped, awaited them. The Princess was given a silver-headed arrow flighted with peacock feathers before they galloped off in pursuit of the red deer; at the hunt's end the helpless buck was held tight as Elizabeth cut its throat. It was a more vivid and a crueller age. When her half-sister, Queen Mary, visited Elizabeth at Hatfield they went straight from divine service to watch a savage display of bear-baiting 'with which their Highnesses were right well content'. But Sir Thomas Pope, Elizabeth's kindly jailor during her enforced stay at Hatfield, laid on less bloodthirsty entertainments like the Shrovetide masque in 1556, when the Great Hall of the Palace rang with the music of minstrels and glowed with the crimson satin, gold and pearls of the guests at a banquet of 70 dishes.

For centuries huntsmen rode out from Hatfield to kill the deer, the fox and the game bird. Lady Emily, 1st Marchioness of Salisbury, was first Mistress of the Hatfield Hounds and Dog Kennel Lane in the New Town notes where her pack was kept. In 1789 she held the first meeting of the Hertfordshire Archers at Hatfield House, another shining scene with the ladies in their uniforms of green coats, beaver hats with a gold band and white medallions embroidered with a gold bow and arrow. There was a remarkable slaughter of Hatfield Park's partridge population on 1 September 1835 when Lord Salisbury wagered Sir John Sebright that four men, using a single gun, could kill 100 brace in a day. Passing the gun from hand to hand, the marksmen reached their target in some five hours, the last shot, Frederick Delme Radcliffe, a noted huntsman, bringing down 36 birds in three quarters of an hour.

Over the centuries, the townsfolk followed a traditional cycle of Saints' Days and seasonal festivals with Maypoles, bonfires and merrymaking. The gentlemen of Hertfordshire and Middlesex engaged in one of many cock-fighting contests in March 1783 and afterwards lunched at the Eight Bells. In September 1838 the Hertfordshire Agricultural Society held its first annual meeting at Hatfield, starting with a ploughing match at Astwick Farm and ending with dinner for 200 in the Red Lion, with Lord Salisbury in the chair. For many years the annual Herts Show was held in Hatfield Park.

The game of cricket has long associations with the town. On 23 September 1789 the first known match — a single wicket game between two gentlemen of Hatfield and two from Bedfordshire — was played for a purse of 50 guineas, which Hatfield won, and the following year a Hatfield side played a Hertfordshire XI at Wadesmill. Since those 18th century summers, every season has seen cricket at Hatfield. In 1818 there were four games against county sides, Hatfield winning and losing twice. In the victorious matches

Hatfield had the advantage of one of the greatest of all cricketers on their side, the Reverend Lord Frederick Beauclerk. Son of the 5th Duke of St Albans and great-great grandson of Charles II and Nell Gwynne, he was one of the first great amateur cricketers and President of the MCC in 1826. Lord Cranborne, later the 2nd Marquess of Salisbury, also played for the town in 1818. Towards the end of the 19th century a commercial traveller named Walter Brearley was confined to bed at the Red Lion for three weeks with measles. As he recovered, he was persuaded to join Hatfield Cricket Club and was in the side for the annual match at Lord's against the Cross Arrows team of groundstaff in 1897. Brearley went on to play for Lancashire and Cheshire, the nearest Hatfield has come to producing a potential Test player.

Until 1923 the town club remained on the traditional pitch in the Park, then it had to move to make way for the Hatfield Estate Cricket Club for employees of the Cecil family. The town club went to play at the Showfield ground in what is now Clarkes Road and in 1928 moved to the new Stonecross Road Athletic Ground with other of the town's sportsmen. In 1946 it returned to the Park, merging with the Estate Club, the separate names eventually blending into Hatfield Cricket Club again in 1976.

One of the greatest of contemporary cricketers has a passing association with Hatfield. In June 1956 Denis Compton played his first game after a leg operation for a Lord Salisbury's XI captained by his great partner W. J. Edrich, who lived in Hatfield at the time and was a Vice President of the Hatfield club. Played despite the rain, the game was more notable for the distinguished reputation of its players than for any cricketing significance. The dashing Compton hit 82 in forty five minutes.

After nearly 200 summers, cricket will soon no longer be played in the beautiful setting behind Hatfield House. The growing traffic of tourists has meant that future wickets will fall on a new pitch provided by the Marquess of Salisbury at Ascots Lane. It will be the end of a long, golden over.

One of the few Royal Tennis courts in England was built by the Fore Street entrance to Hatfield Park by the 2nd Marquess of Salisbury in 1843. Joseph Lambert became the marker or professional in 1849 and his five sons, having learned the game at Hatfield, went on to become markers themselves. One son, George, was world champion from 1871-85 and another, Charles, took over his father's post at Hatfield. W. A. 'Jack' Groom, born in Fore Street, was marker at Hatfield before becoming Head Professional at the Lord's club. He returned to Hatfield in 1955 and helped to start the Hatfield House Tennis Club, which still flourishes. The club has the well-worn racket used by the 3rd Marquess of Salisbury, its longer handle designed to compensate for lack of nimbleness in later years.

The Herts Croquet and Lawn Tennis Club, formed in 1897, played at Kennelwood Lane; the Hatfield Tennis Club had courts on what is now the Ryde Estate. In 1921 the two amalgamated and, after one of the croquet lawns had been converted to a bowling green, they became the Hatfield Lawn Tennis and Bowling Club in 1924. Teddy Higgs, the singles champion 1922-24, played at Wimbledon and represented England in the Davis Cup. In 1965 the club moved to College Lane, Roe Green, where its facilities now include an indoor bowling green.

The Stonecross Road ground to which the cricketers moved in 1928 was also the home of the Athletic Club and Hatfield Town Football Club; the former and its various associated sporting activities vanished just before the war but the soccer club, founded in the 1890s, survived through troubled times. With an average home attendance of 142 in 1955, the secretary said the club had a 'committee of nobodies' and would perish because no well-known people would help to run it. Having survived the subsequent 22 years, the club again faced extinction in 1977 when the Welwyn Hatfield District Council wanted its ground for housing. The future seemed even gloomier than in 1955.

Before the First World War, the 4th Marquess of Salisbury laid down a private 18-hole golf course in Hatfield Park which was also used by people in the town. It fell into disuse about the time of the Second World War and there is today nowhere to play golf in Hatfield.

With a new indoor swimming pool built for the town, Hatfield Rural District Council launched a swimming club in 1966. Enthusiasm rapidly bred a competitive team, a growing list of county and national honours and individual selection for international competitions. With Kelvin Juba as full time professional coach since 1973, the club now has some 450 members.

The Hatfield School of Music and Drama was founded in 1960 and three years later Hatfield Drama was formed out of it. Under the continuing direction of Doris Day, this has provided an outlet for amateur theatre talent and occasionally a first step towards the professional stage. The Hatfield Symphony Orchestra first played in 1961 and disbanded in 1969, the year the Hatfield Philharmonic, based at Hatfield Polytechnic, emerged under its first conductor, Frank Shipway. The same year saw the Mid Herts Music Centre move from Welwyn Garden City to the Burleigh School, with Peter Haskins as Advisory Teacher of Music. Starting with five pupils, the centre now has 1,000 student visits a week.

Since 1958 there have been weekly jazz concerts at the Red Lion which have attracted many famous American traditional jazz players and in July 1977 the Mid Herts Youth Orchestra performed the first concert in the town's new (and costly) leisure centre, The Forum. It stands close to what had been Hatfield's only cinema, once the Odeon, later the Curzon, which has followed the pattern of late 20th century pleasurable pursuits and become a bingo hall.

Coursing in Hatfield Park in the 18th century.

Hatfield cricketers, 1865 vintage, and INSET: the Reverend Lord
Frederick Beauclerk.

ABOVE: Hatfield Cricket Club in the 1920s. BELOW: The 1897 team that played the Cross Arrows at Lords. Brearley's name has been mis-spelt.

111

ABOVE: The summer of 1977: Hatfield playing on the pitch which first saw a game of cricket in 1789. BELOW: Lord Salisbury with his XI for Compton's come-back match in June 1956, and INSET: Compton in action. The umpire is Bert Shepherd.

The Old Palace as stables. (CRO)

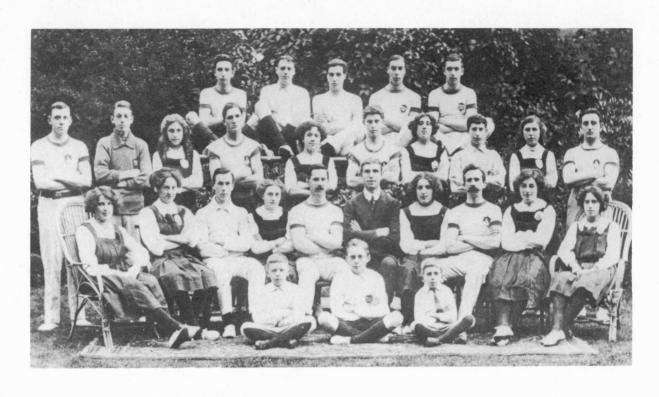

ABOVE: Hatfield Athletic Club in 1910. BELOW: Hatfield Town FC,
Bingham-Cox cup winners 1909-10.

114

ABOVE: The public hall where talkies were first shown in Hatfield in 1933. (CNT) BELOW: The Odeon cinema, closed in 1973, now a bingo hall. (JF)

ABOVE: Lord Baden-Powell (right) inspecting scouts at a county rally in
Hatfield Park in July 1933. BELOW: The Forum leisure centre.

116

ABOVE: Hatfield Philharmonic, conducted by Frank Shipway, rehearsing with 'cellist Paul Tortelier and his son in July 1974. (WHT)
BELOW: American jazzman Wild Bill Davison playing at the Red Lion in 1975. (DW)

117

Hatfield set to music in the 19th century. (CC)

Brave New World

Nearly 1,000 years ago, when the Domesday Book was compiled, there were some 300 people in Hatfield. Today that figure has grown a hundredfold and the greatest increase has come in the last 30 years since Hatfield was designated a New Town in 1948, a decision brought about by the housing demands of the growing De Havilland workforce.

In those 30 years, largely under the direction of the Commission for the New Towns, tower blocks, modern estates and a shopping centre precinct have been laid down to the west of the railway line, the building of which led to the creation of the first Hatfield New Town in the 1850s. The St Albans Road has been severed and a giant Woolco department store now stands square across its line. What was for centuries simply called Hatfield is now defined as the Old Town — and much of that is now new.

To the north lies Welwyn Garden City, a sometimes uneasy bedfellow since local government reshaping in 1974 brought the two towns within the jurisdiction of one district council. Such matters are the latest and not the last adjustments in ten centuries of change, once gradual, now more sudden, as we continue to pursue our strange, eventful history.

The disappearing St Albans Road, right, as the town centre is redeveloped.

A final look through the windows of the cottages that stood on the site of Woolco store. (JF)

ABOVE: Woolco under construction. (CNT) BELOW: Briars Lane in the 1950s. The swimming pool now stands about where the building on the right is. (JH)

121

...re Street in celebration, first for ...e 1909 visit of Edward VII and then ...: in November 1974 for ...al Heritage Year. (JF) BELOW: ...atfield New Town, about the time ...World War. RIGHT ABOVE: Park ...om the bridge leading into Hatfield ...) and BELOW CENTRE: the view ...me point today. RIGHT: Modern Hatfield from the air.

Hatfield shopping precinct. (JF)

Brave New World.

Appendix

Written on the flyleaf of a Gospel book belonging to the Diocese of Ely, this manuscript in the British Library is almost certainly older than the Domesday Book and is the earliest known written record concerning Hatfield still in existence. Translated from the Anglo Saxon with modern place-names, it reads:

'Dudda was a Hatfield serf. He had three daughters. One was called Deorwyn, the second was Deorswyth and the third was called Golda. Wullaf of Hatfield married Deorwyn; Aelfstan at Datchworth took Deorswyth as his wife and Ealhstan, Aelfstan's brother, married Golda.

A man named Hwita was a beekeeper at Hatfield and Tate, his daughter, was the mother of Wulfsig. A man called Lulle married Wulsig's sister Hehstan and they lived in Walden.

Wifus and Dunne and Seoloce were born on the estate in Hatfield. Wifus's son Duding is settled at Walden. Dunne's son, called Ceolmund, is also settled at Walden. Seoloce's son, called Atheleah, is also settled at Walden. Tate has Cenwald's sister May for his wife at Welwyn. Ealdelm, son of Aerethrythe, had Tate's daughter as a wife. Waerstan's father, called Waerlaf, was a Hatfield dweller (literally 'property of the Hatfield estate') and kept the grey swine.

Brada was a Hatfield serf. Hwite, Brada's wife, was the daughter of a Hatfield serf. This Hwite was the mother of Waerstan and Waerthrythe and Wynburg. And this Waerstan was settled at Watton and had Winne's sister for his wife. Wine has Waerthrythe as a wife. Dunne, who was brought up on the estate at Hatfield, lived at Watton. Her daughter, called Deorwyn, was married to Cynewald at Munden. Her brother, called Deornath, is with Cynewald. Wifus's daughter, called Dudda, is settled at Wymondeley. Cenwald's father, called Cynelm, was a serf of the Hatfield estate. Cenwald's son, called Manna, is settled at Watton-under-Eadwolde(?).

A woman called Buhe was Dryhtlaf's maternal aunt: She departed from Hatfield to Essendon. There were three sisters, Athelwyn, Eadug and Athelgyth. Tilewine and Duda were both the children of Buge. Ealhstan was the son of Tilewine, Wulfsig was the son of Eadug. Ceole was the son of Athelgyth. Ceolstan and Manwine were offspring of Felda. Deorulf, Cyneburgh's son and his two sisters. Cynric and Clavering, their uncle. Those men are relatives of Tata, the Hatfield serf.'

(Picture reproduced by permission of the British Library Board. Manuscript is Cotton MS. Tiberius B V, part 1, f. 76v.)

Sources and Bibliography

Hatfield and its People by various authors. (Workers' Education Association 1959-64)
The Cecils of Hatfield House by Lord David Cecil. (Constable and Company Ltd 1973)
Bishop's Hatfield by Jocelyn J. Antrobus.
Liber Eliensis edited by Dr E. O. Blake. (Royal Historical Society Camden Series)
Handbook to the Land Charters and other Saxonic Documents by John Earle. (Clarendon Press 1888)
The Book of Welwyn by Richard Busby. (Barracuda Books 1976)
D. H. An outline of De Havilland history by C. Martin Sharp. (Faber and Faber 1960)
Sky Fever by Sir Geoffrey de Havilland. (Hamish Hamilton 1961)
The Tale of the Comet by Derek D. Dempster. (Allan Wingate 1959)
Hertfordshire by W. Branch Johnson. (B. T. Batsford 1970)
Old Hertfordshire Calendar by Doris Jones-Baker. (Phillimore 1974)
The Folklore of Hertfordshire by Doris Jones-Baker. (B. T. Batsford 1977)
The Later Cecils by Kenneth Rose. (Weidenfeld and Nicolson 1975)
The Church Bells of Hertfordshire by Thomas North and J. C. L. Stahlschmidt.
The Sports and Pastimes of England by Joseph Strutt.
Dictionary of National Biography.
Tanks 1914-1918 Logbook of a Pioneer by Sir Albert G. Stern. (Hodder and Stoughton 1919)
A history of the English Church and People by the Venerable Bede, translated by Leo Sherley-Price, revised by R. E. Latham. (Penguin Books 1977)
Place Names of Hertfordshire. (English Place-Names Society)
Hatfield and District Archaeological Society Journal, various volumes.
Welwyn and Hatfield Times, various editions.
Hertfordshire Inns by W. Branch Johnson. (Herts Countryside 1962)
Victoria County History and the Clutterbuck and Chauncy County Histories.

Salisbury Manuscripts, various volumes. (Her Majesty's Stationery Office)
Cecil Family Papers, transcribed and edited by R. T. Gunton.
Hatfield Parish Council Records.
Hertford County Session Rolls, various volumes. (Herts County Council)
Calendar of Assize Records, Hertfordshire Indictments for the reigns of Elizabeth I and James I. (Her Majesty's Stationery Office)

Index

Subscribers

Presentation copies

1 Hatfield Parish Council
2 The Most Hon. The Marquess of Salisbury
3 British Aerospace
4 Welwyn Hatfield District Council
5 Herts County Council
6 Hatfield Library

7 Robert Richardson
8 Clive Birch
9 Miss Margaret Grace
   Pritchard
10 Kenneth Henry
   Hutchinson
11 Geoffrey J. Turner
12 J. R. Alcock
13 Richard Wittingham
14 Mrs M. Pollard
15 Peter Joseph Mallett
16 Mrs J. Clark
17 J. Clark
18 Fred & Eileen Tucker
19 Ray & Claire
   Penstone-Smith
20 H. M. Sawyer
21 John Dean
22 Mrs J. Malcolm
23 Herts County Library
28 Headquarters
29 Mrs D. E. Stevens
30 J. Higgins
31 Mrs S. Chapman
32 Dr & Mrs E. I. Sherrard
33 Mrs Ida Thomas
34 S. C. Randall
35 Mrs E. Hyslop
36 Peter Chard
37 W.H.B. Cash
38 A. D. Kingstone
39 Miss Patricia Everett
40 Mr & Mrs M. Dias
41 P. Jervis
42 R.J. Busby
43 Miss B. M. Harrison
44 R. B. Coleman
45 Albert William Cox
46 Mr & Mrs A. P.
   Holland
47 Hatfield Public
55 Library
56 S. M. Cunningham
57 Mr & Mrs H. R. Lane
58 Rev M. B. & Mrs West
59 Donald H. Cordwell
60 Miss R. D. Thorne
61 Miss A. J. Wallace
62 V. J. Cull
63 J. G. Hall
64 Cllr Frank Clayton
65 A. F. Smith
66 G. F. Carpenter
67 Henry W. Gray
68 C. H. Gansert
79 Mrs D. A. Model
70 J. R. Garwood
71 Mrs E. M. Tuohy
72 A. W. Macey
73 R. K. Smith
74 K. W. Seaman
75 E. F. Cull
76 Doris M. Day
77 Gerald A. Roberts
78 Dr & Mrs A. M. Roe
79 Ron Grey
80 Commission for the
89 New Towns
90 T. W. Adamson
91 Mrs F. Page
92 Mrs M. Jenkinson
93 Mrs D. Hickson
94 R. Dixon
95 Mrs E. M. Jenkins
96 J. H. Hunt
97 Miss Helen Campbell
98 Robin Sedley
99 J. A. Bancroft
100 Mrs E. G. Kewn
101 Mrs S. D. Robson
102 Mrs E. Webb
103 R. J. Ainsworth
104 Mrs Soanes
105 R. G. Redding

106 Mrs M. English
107 A. J. Stanbury
108 F. F. Horgan
109 G. H. Bailey
110 W. L. Ashfield
111 Onslow School
112 Mrs G. Brown
113 Mrs E. A. Mansfield
114 Peter Dawson
115 Mrs Y. J. Thomas
116 W. M. Morley
117 R. H. Harcourt
   Williams
118 Mr & Mrs B. G.
   Gearing
119 D. R. Howard
120 Roger Fisher
121 John Partridge
122 John Lingham-French
123 Colin R. Vickers
124 Aileen Patricia Farmer
125 Mrs A. Weston
126 A. W. Parker
127 C. D. Everard
128 Colin J. Evans
129 Mrs F. I. Godfrey
130 C. E. Clough
131 Mrs J. Dollimore
132 Mrs I. Cox
133 Mrs J. J. Radford
134 B. Wright
135 P. J. Mullin
136 P. J. Freeman
137 H. J. Wentworth
138 Mrs P. Clark
139 H. Parrott
140 Mrs A. Gilroy
141 Joan & Tony
   Lammiman
142 Terry & Eileen
   O'Dowd
143 Mr & Mrs Christopher
   Clark
144 K. Towson
145 Hatfield Parish
   Council
146 Zierikzee Town
   Council
147 D. R. Shrimpton
148 L. J. Silver
149 Mrs E. F. Jarvis
150 G. Bubb
151 Dennis G. Bodman
152 F. Cobb
153 Anita & Anthony
   Hoyle
154 Mrs Rosemary H. J.
   Basden
155 C. G. Day
156 M. F. Yearsley
157 Mr & Mrs T. & M.
   Bishop
158 Mrs Ethel Wheeler
159 J. E. Mileham
160 A. W. Scott
   Rutherford
161 Mahnaz Motamenpour
162 W. M. Millichamp
163 Bill & Ivy Hough
164 Eric & Mary Tingey

165 Francis Knight
166 John & Suzanne
   Brown
167 Mr & Mrs L. C.
   Mardell
168 A. W. Denchfield
169 E. J. Tomlin
170 K. Long
171 B. Clark
172 B. J. Smith
173 L. A. Worrell
174 Mrs Kathleen
   Chorlton
175 Rosemary E.
   Dudgeon
176 A. J. Upson
177 John Winder
178 John Hembury
179 E. Whitbread
180 Mrs P. B. Wass
181 F. Combeer
182 Susan Lenahan
183 J. J. Fallon
184 Hatfield School
185 Mr & Mrs H.
   Ditchfield
186 Susan Truman
187 Miss A. Gover
188 Miss S. M. Turner
189 Janet Robinson
190 K. Webb
191 E. Vaughan
192 Donald J. Munro
193 Liz Mence
194 G. E. Relph
195 R. A. Richardson
196 Beorge Boyes
197 Norma Fulford
198 Janet Miller
199 Mr & Mrs Hall
200 Peter Lawrence
201 J. W. Tyler
202 P. Brook
230 Mrs D. J. Papworth
204 I. Oram
205 E. R. H. Simmonds
206 Christopher Hackett
207 Mrs S. R. Hulks
208 Ethel Thomas
209 C. F. Groom
210 Mrs R. Hart
211 Mrs C. P. Martin
212 Mr & Mrs C. L.
   Christiansen
213 Mr & Mrs W. F. Edlin
214 Mr & Mrs Swan
215 Miss J. Roberts
216 V. T. Palmer
217 Eric & Anne
   Trudgill
218 Constance R.
   Scofield
219 Mr & Mrs J. G.
   Greenfield
220 Martin J. Hall
221 Mrs M. P. Pike
222 Miss J.D. Davies
223 Mrs P. Halsey
224 F. R. Iddiols
225 Mrs L. G. Wright

226 John Brown
227 Pauline Stirk
228 Mrs E. Tipping
229 G. Cooper
230 F. H. Marsden
231 Mrs Vera M. Morgan
232 F. J. Long
233 P.E. Heady
234 K. Casserly
235 E. Pateman
236 Amy Forbes
237 Mrs Eileen M.
   Jordan
238 Ronald & Margaret
   Woodley
239 R. R. McKee
240 W. L. Daeche
241 Mrs M. Castle
242 R. J. Missing
243 S. G. H. Clark
244 Mrs I. McKeown
245 H. Muncey
246 Mrs S. Breame
247 Miss K. R. Halsey
248 Mr & Mrs M. J.
   Osborne
249 R. Russell-Smith
250 W. H. T. Jenner
251 A. P. Roberts
252 G. Mussard
253 Mrs Ruby Chennells
254 Miss V. E. Allen
255 Bryan R. Archer
256 Z. Geeson
257 Mrs O. M. Hinchcliffe
258 Mrs M. Marlborough
259 Paul Jansz
260 Ellis Panton
261 A. W. Wyatt
262 Mrs A. K. Paris
263 B. H. Hurt
264 Cyril Golder
265 S. A. T. Young
266 J. E. Scott
267 Philip J. Birtles
268 G. Thorneycroft
269 D. H. Hulks
270 H. T. Starling
271 J. Simpson
272 Mrs E. A. Morris
273 J. Darragh
274 Mrs W. Denning
275 A. A. Smithson
276 Mrs King
277 Mrs V. A. Shepard
278 Sherrardswood
   School
279 A. H. N. Wells
280 Mrs C. Murray
281 Mrs M. Lee
282 Mrs W. H. Cheer
283 Mrs J. A. Brennan
284 R. J. Keatley
285 Edgar Howard
286 Brenda Margaret
   Shorten
287 Mrs D. E. Ansell
288 John M. Pennington
289 Miss D. R. Edwards
290 W. H. Clegg
291 Joan, Karen, Ian,
   Annette & Neils B.
   Christensen
292 Betty & Allan Davis
293 Robert Dalgarno
294 Dr & Mrs J. P. Dymoke
295 J. A. Bell
296 Mrs G. V. Berrie
297 Gary Dowie
298 Sharon Dowie
299 John Hardy
300 Mr & Mrs R. J. Tingey
301 Zillah & Robert
   Chapman

302 Henry & Kate Mason
303 Paul & Carole Roach
304 M. D. H. Rosenthal
305 George Wenham
306 George Martin
307 Greta & Ronald Bishop
308 Bishops Hatfield Girls' School
309 Miss M. Ashworth
310 Mrs R. Kuntze
311 A. L. Young
312 Steven W. Jones
313 Paul Barnes
314 Herts County
315 Record Office
316 Mr & Mrs T. R. Walters
317 Mr & Mrs T. R. Walters
318 Mr & Mrs E. C. Springham
319 John R. I. Hind
320 I. N. Jenkins
321 B. J. Sarson
322 Mr & Mrs Hentall
323 Mr & Mrs J. Lance
324 John Burgess
325 R. J. Eaton
326 Stanley Huckle
327 Miss E. Binstead
328 Miss L. S. Bristo
329 B. G. Lawrence
330 Miss Jacqueline Smith
331 Moira & John Hill
332 John Michael Reed
333 Trevor Lay
334 Mr & Mrs William Bryceland
335 Mrs F. M. Howe
336 S. F. J. Howe
337 Mrs J. Haniford
338 Anna Todd
339 Alexandra Todd
340 Norman Tuxworth
341 Miss M. I. Allardyce
342 Mr & Mrs J. P. T. Swan
343 Mrs M. M. Kappes
344 R. J. Bushnell
345 R. L. N. Hewson
346 E. Lewis
347 D. Hodson
348 R. V. Jiggens
349 D. Woodhouse
350 Rev John B. Brown
351 Mrs H. M. Richardson
352 Miss Y. Walsingham
353 D. C. Woollett
354 J. F. Parsons
355 Miss Patrician M. Dunham
356 P. R.Lucas
357 A. J. Shepherdson
358 Mrs Pamela Sherriff
359 Miss Norah Sherriff
360 John Mardling
361 R. W. Parrott
362 Mr & Mrs David Nickell
363 D. C. Hartley
364 P. M. Attridge
365 D. J. Hyde
366 Mrs I. Tempest
367 R. J. Kidd
368 Edward Emsley
369 G. Hill
370 Mrs V. A. Reeves
371 Mrs J. Cast
372 C. Baldock
373 Mr & Mrs E. D. Watts
374 Mr & Mrs G. D. Watts
375 Mrs M. Matthews

376 Mrs P. R. O. Storey
377 Panshanger JMI School
378 Mr & Mrs J. R. Little
379 Mrs T. Parker
380 Derborah Dow
381 Caroline Dow
382 Mike & Andrea Emery
383 Chris Pearcey
384 Jack Waters
385 D. E. Markee
386 Monks Walk School
387 Chancellor's School
388
389 Onslow School
390 Richard Paul Lloyd
391 Countess Anne School
392 Mr & Mrs D. L. Hoy
393 P. W. Barrows
394 Kelvin Juba
395 Miss M. A. Cooper
396 C. J. G. Parish
397 Howlands School
398 A. M. Foster
399 Mrs Edith E. Roden
400 Dr E. H. J. Cotter
401 K. W. Budge
402 B. R. Archer; Archer, Boxer, Partners
403 Kewbury Ltd.
404 Holwell JMI School
405 Mrs E. B. Williams
406 J. M. Davison
407 B. Curtis
408 Maurice John Baldwin
409
410 J. C. Watson
411 R. M. Bailey
412 Arthur Rollings
413 Glyn Jones
414 F. T. Stephenson
415 Mrs E. Hayes
416 R. J. Poole
417 Shirley & Norman Knapp
418 Dave Berberian
419 T. Maling
420 Mr & Mrs Dale Emery
421 Miss Sheila M. Graham
422 E. J. G. Balley
423 Mrs Irene Lee
424 Mr & Mrs R. L. Helmore
425 The Chairman, Welwyn Hatfield District Council
426 Mr & Mrs R. P. Palmer
427
428 D. W. L. Eccles
429 Humphrey Whitbread
430 Malcolm J. Scott
431 Mrs Sue M. Fry
432 Hatfield & District Archaeological Society
433 H. J. J. King
434 Hemel Hempstead
436 Library
437 Frederick Jack Parker
438 C. V. Brutey
439 Heronswood School
440 St Audrey's School
441 Kenilworth School
442 Green Lanes JMI School
443 Graham R. Phillips
444 R. Tott
445 A. E. Cooper
446 F. H. Curtis
447 David Howard Thompson

449 R. P. Kingdon
450 Mrs J. M. Pallett
451 Christopher J. Harrison
452 R. Smith
453 Miss J.E. Bailey
454 M. Greenham
455 Peter John Davis
456 I.K. Greygoose
457 James Seeby
485 John Hall
459 Mrs H. Hooker
460 Mrs D. Angell
461 D. K. Davies
462 Kings Langley School
463 Gwen Robinson
464 C. R. Hills
465 Bryan Lilley
466 Leslie Asquith
467 F. Prescott
468 Mrs A. Aslett
469 A. L. Roads
470
471 D. Sutcliffe
472 Millwards Junior School
473 Mrs Ruth H. R. Rawson
474 Mr Paul English &
475 Mrs E. English
476 Mrs Joan I. Adams
477 Mrs Gladys Chard
478 D. G. Mackie
479 Joseph Cooper
480 David Cooper
481 M. Callen
482 Mrs M. C. King
483 Dr D. A. Lewis
484 John P. B. Clarke
485
486 E. C. Meredith
488 G. E. Lancaster
487 Mrs J. Hall
488 G. E. Lancaster
489 Mrs P. Frost
490 Mrs P. W. Lomas
491 Miss Marian Benton
492 Victoria & Albert Museum
493 John L. Harris
494 Mr & Mrs R. J. Morgan
495 Mrs Patricia P. Parsons
496 W. G. Douglas
494 Mrs Edna Wilding
498 Mrs P. Tomey
499 Miss J. Lee
500
501 Mr L. P. Hodge
502 M. D. Greenacre
503 Mrs Muriel Walker
504 Mrs Doris Joyce Banham
505 P. W. Barrows
506 Mrs Mary R. Moore
507 National Westminster Bank Ltd
508 Philip Eames
509 Mrs L. Whitehouse
510 Miss I. D. Woolving
511 L. M. Sargent
512 F. W. Vann
513 John Bauch
514 G. M. Goscomb
515 J. Groom
516 C. E. J. Brown
517 British Aerospace
528 Aircraft Group
529 Mr & Mrs G. S. Brown
530 Mr & Mrs C. J. N. Miller
531 Michael J. Richardson

532 James M. Richardson
533 Richard Chancellor Male
534 Rev & Mrs B. P. Moore
535 David & Anne Hughes
536 Ben Gunn
537 Mrs E. J. Gudgeon
538 V. Sullivan
539 Mr & Mrs Paul Barnes
540 Mrs S. J. Noad
541 B. T. Whincap
542 Mr & Mrs L. Miller
543 Mr & Mrs S. Kemp
544 John Kernaghan
545 C. J. Chapman
546 Mrs J. Rackstraw
547 Denis J. Williams
548 Mrs Angela Axbey
549 John Lindon Munday
550 Mrs J. L. R. Cole
551 Mr & Mrs Stewart
552 Philip James Porter
553 Neil Collins
554 Mr & Mrs J. J. Burgess, Kym, Anna, Carl & Michele
555 Mr & Mrs Leonard Dollimore
556 Heather M. Brickley
557 Mr & Mrs I. Taylor
558 C. Smith
559 Stanley & Christine Neale
560 George P. Steell
561 C. C. & J. C. Hanson
562 Clifford & Nancy Greatrex
563 Mrs Peggy James
564 Miss P. Rogers
565 David P. Clabour
566 Kenneth W. Miller
567 Eric Hill
568 Geoffrey & Jean Pritchard
569 Wild Bill & Anne Davison
570 Mr & Mrs S. A. J. King
571 Mrs Margaret Toose
572 Mr H. K. & Mrs S. G. Lee
573 Brenda Weeden
574 Mr & Mrs J. Beenstock
575 Colette, Marcel, Nathalie & Jean-Philippe Glaskie
576 Mrs J. Parker
577 Mr & Mrs Harold White
578 Mr & Mrs Dale Robinson
579 Rev G. Webb
580 David & Rosemary Shirley
581 Mrs J. Richardson
582 Mr & Mrs Bolitho
583 Roy A. Hicks
584 Mr & Mrs A. E. H. Antell
585 Mrs Constance Cater
586 Mrs Hiscock
587 Welwyn & Hatfield Times
588 J. Hayton
589 Mrs Judith Pearson
590 Roger, Janet, Sara, Clare Freeman
591 St Philip Howard School
592 D. Brewster
593 Mr & Mrs W. A. Fox
594 C. Lavender
595 Mr & Mrs R. H. Perry
596 Ian Peter Andrews
597 Mrs P. D. Brown
598 Howard Richards
599 J. Trevor Jones

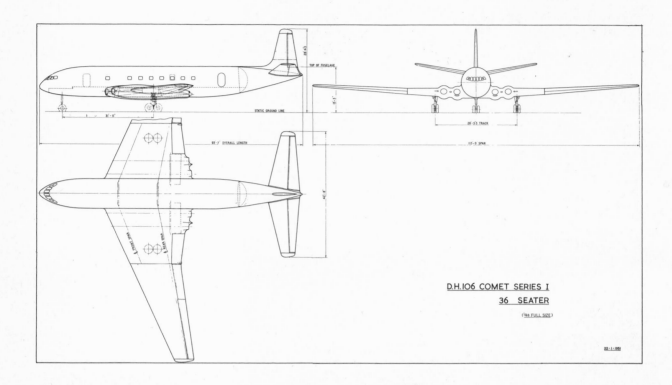

D.H.106 COMET SERIES I

36 SEATER

(¼₈ FULL SIZE)

22·1·1951

BACK COVER: General assembly drawings of the Comet airliner.

KEY TO CAPTION CREDITS